EASY GUITAR
WITH NOTES & TAB

STEVE MILLER BAND
YOUNG HEARTS COMPLETE GREATEST HITS

T0041093

"Space Intro" and "Threshold" have been omitted due to the absence of guitar.

ISBN 0-634-07725-2

HAL•LEONARD® CORPORATION

7777 W. BLUEMOUND RD. P.O. BOX 13819 MILWAUKEE, WI 53213

Visit Hal Leonard Online at
www.halleonard.com

Steve Miller Band, 1977 (L to R) Lonnie Turner (bass), Greg Douglas (guitar), Byron Allred (keyboards), Steve Miller (guitar), Norton Buffalo (harmonica), Gary Mallaber (drums), David Denny (guitar)

STRUM AND PICK PATTERNS

This chart contains the suggested strum and pick patterns that are referred to by number at the beginning
of each song in this book. The symbols ⊓ and ∨ in the strum patterns refer to down and up strokes, respectively.
The letters in the pick patterns indicate which right-hand fingers plays which strings.

p = thumb
i = index finger
m = middle finger
a = ring finger

For example; Pick Pattern 2
is played: thumb - index - middle - ring

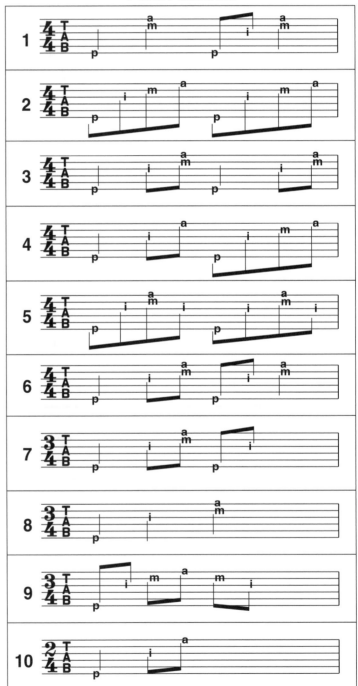

Strum Patterns

Pick Patterns

You can use the 3/4 Strum or Pick Patterns in songs written in compound meter (6/8, 9/8, 12/8, etc.).
For example, you can accompany a song in 6/8 by playing the 3/4 pattern twice in each measure.
The 4/4 Strum and Pick Patterns can be used for songs written in cut time (¢) by doubling the note
time values in the patterns. Each pattern would therefore last two measures in cut time.

Take the Money and Run

Words and Music by Steve Miller

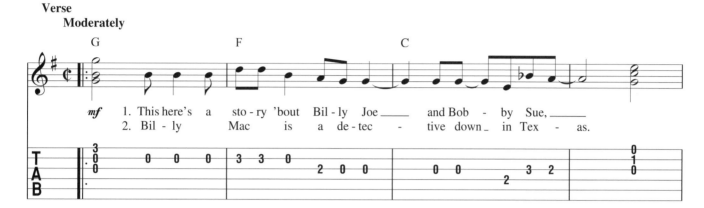

Strum Pattern: 1
Pick Pattern: 3

Verse
Moderately

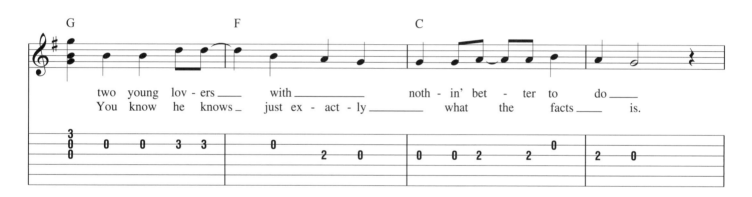

1. This here's a sto - ry 'bout Bil - ly Joe ___ and Bob - by Sue, ___
2. Bil - ly Mac is a de - tec - tive down ___ in Tex - as.

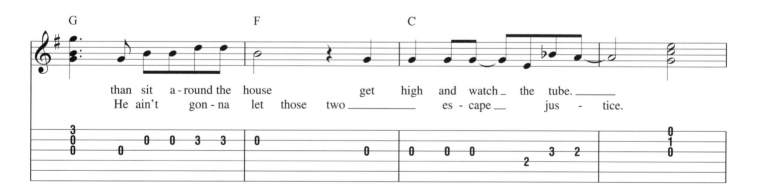

two young lov - ers ___ with ___ noth - in' bet - ter to do ___
You know he knows ___ just ex - act - ly ___ what the facts ___ is.

than sit a - round the house ___ get high and watch ___ the tube. ___
He ain't gon - na let those two ___ es - cape ___ jus - tice.

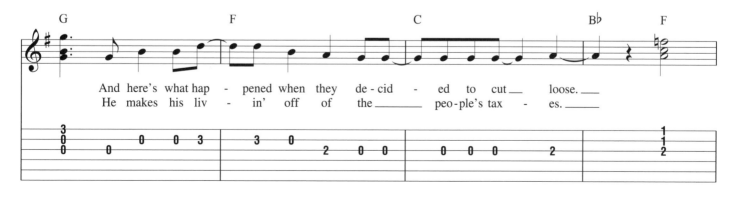

And here's what hap - pened when they de - cid - ed to cut ___ loose. ___
He makes his liv - in' off of the ___ peo - ple's tax - es. ___

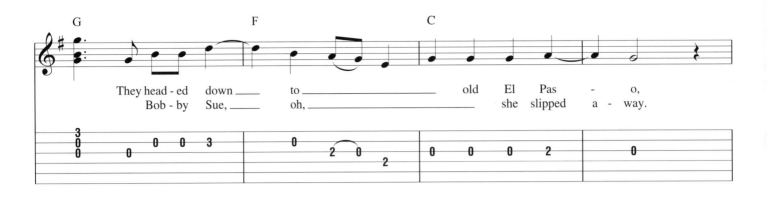

They head-ed down ____ to ____ old El Pas - o,
Bob - by Sue, ____ oh, ____ she slipped a - way.

that's where they ran ____ in - to a great, big has - sle.
Bil - ly Joe ____ caught up to her the ver - y next ____ day.

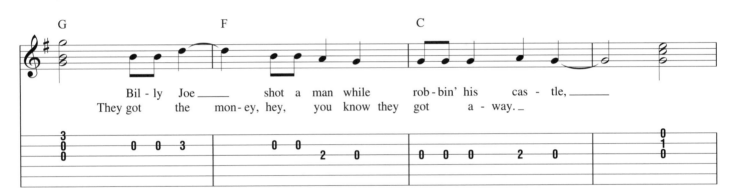

Bil - ly Joe ____ shot a man while rob - bin' his cas - tle, ____
They got the mon - ey, hey, you know they got a - way. ____

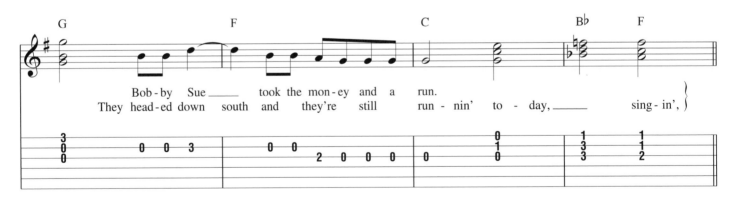

Bob - by Sue ____ took the mon - ey and a run.
They head - ed down south and they're still run - nin' to - day, ____ sing - in',

Chorus

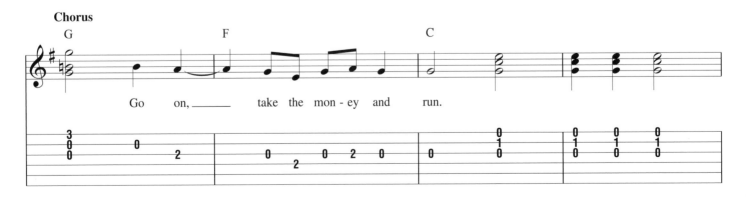

Go on, ____ take the mon - ey and run.

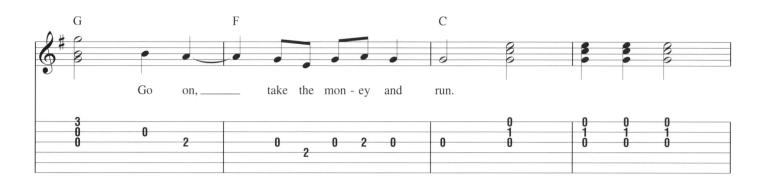

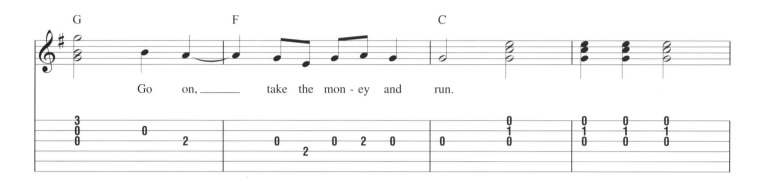

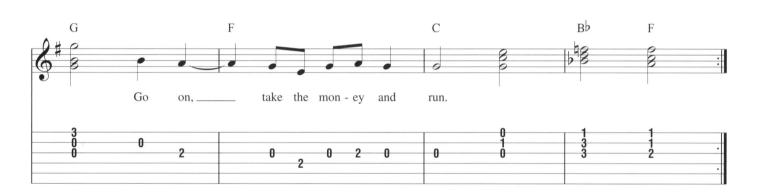

Interlude

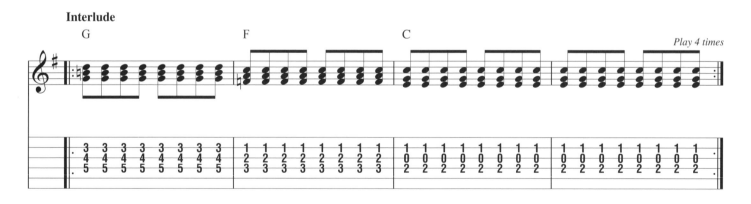

Outro-Chorus

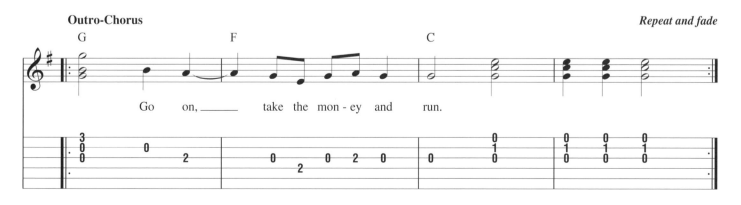

Abracadabra

Words and Music by Steve Miller

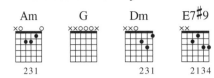

Strum Pattern: 1
Pick Pattern: 1

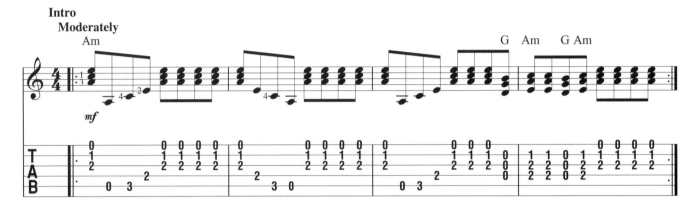

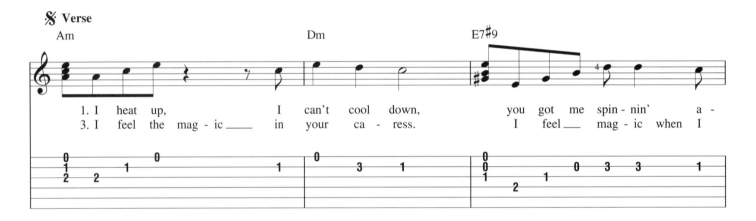

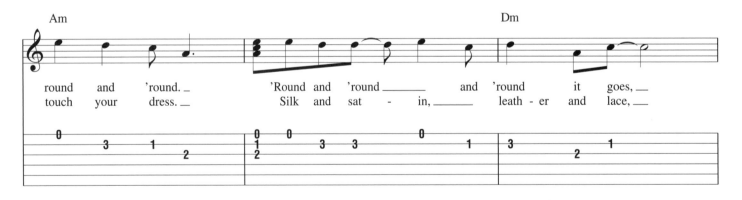

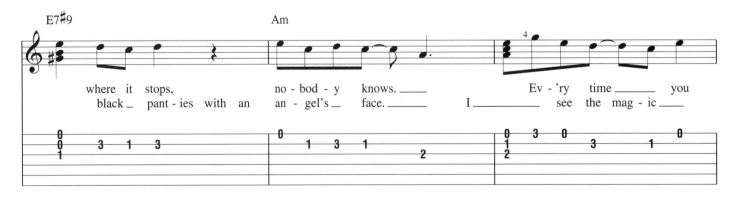

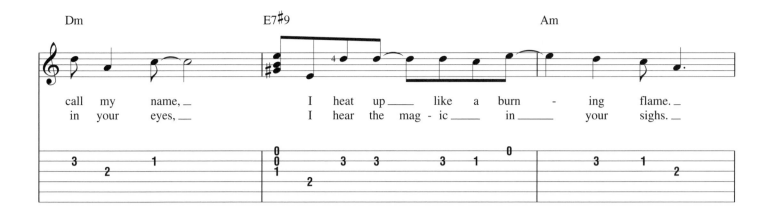

call my name, ___ I heat up ___ like a burn - ing flame. ___
in your eyes, ___ I hear the mag - ic ___ in ___ your sighs. ___

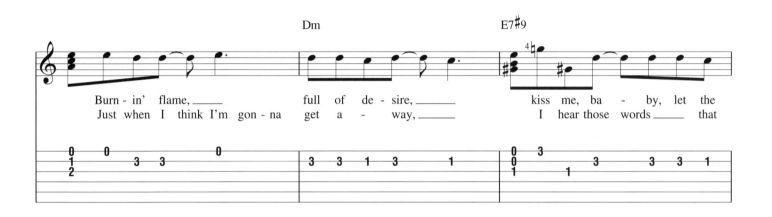

Burn - in' flame, ___ full of de - sire, ___ kiss me, ba - by, let the
Just when I think I'm gon - na get a - way, ___ I hear those words ___ that

Chorus

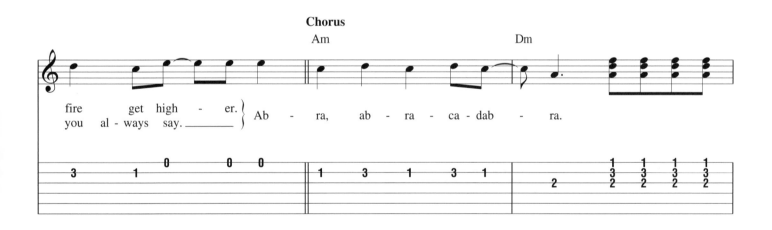

fire get high - er. } Ab - ra, ab - ra - ca - dab - ra.
you al - ways say. ___ }

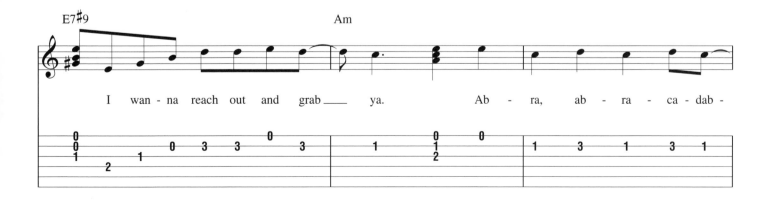

I wan - na reach out and grab ___ ya. Ab - ra, ab - ra - ca - dab -

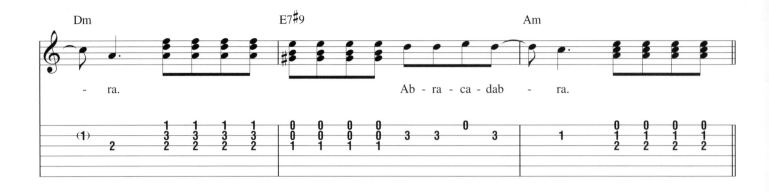

Verse

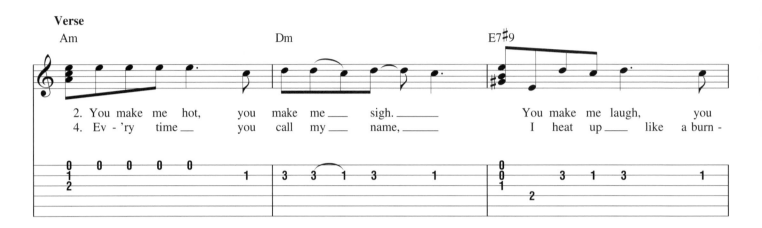

2. You make me hot, you make me ___ sigh. _____ You make me laugh, you
4. Ev - 'ry time ___ you call my ___ name, _____ I heat up ___ like a burn -

To Coda

make me cry. _____ Keep me burn - in' for your love _____
- in' flame. _____ Burn - in' flame, _____ full of de - sire, _____

Chorus

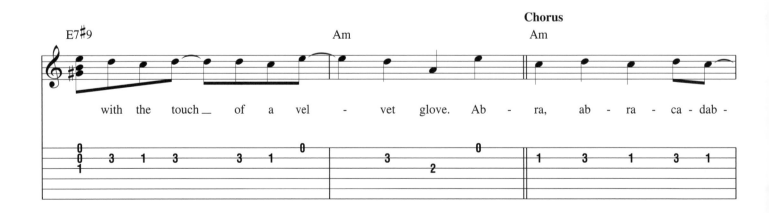

with the touch ___ of a vel - vet glove. Ab - ra, ab - ra - ca - dab -

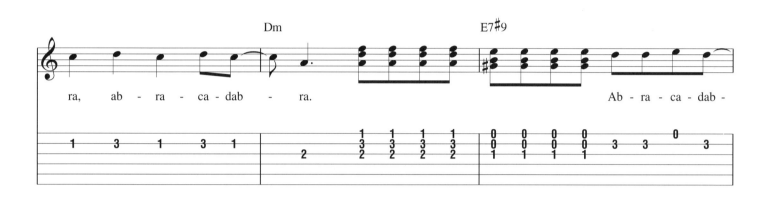

D.S. al Coda   **Coda**

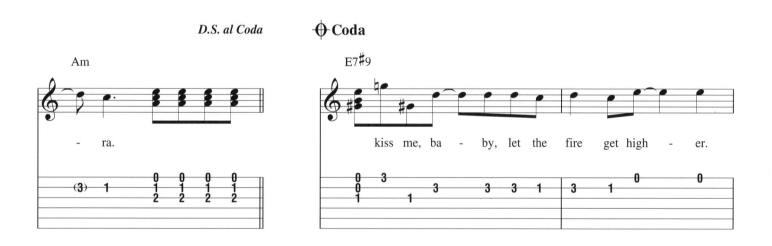

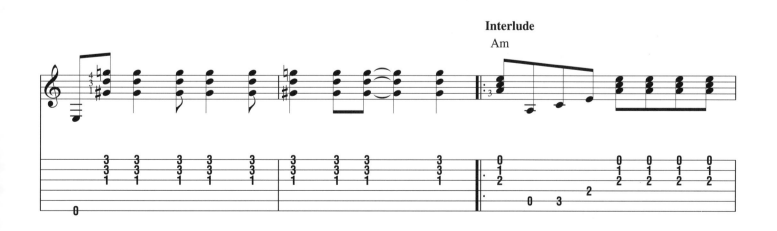

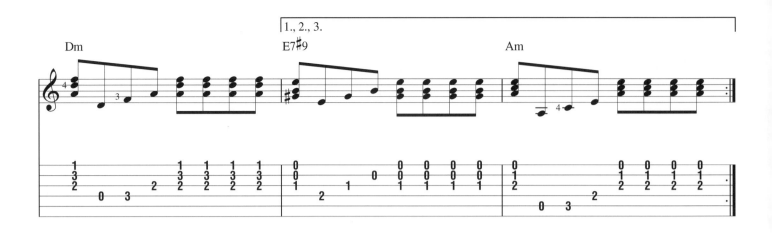

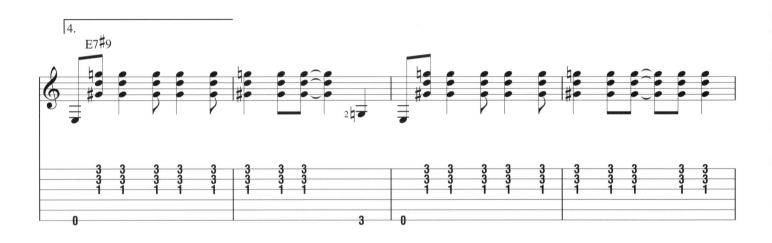

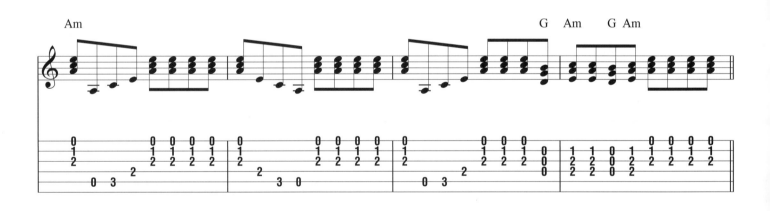

Outro

Repeat and fade

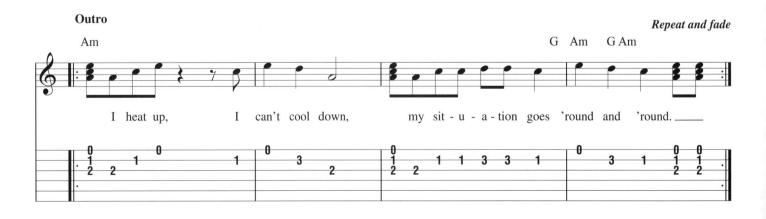

I heat up, I can't cool down, my sit - u - a - tion goes 'round and 'round. _____

Rock'n Me

Words and Music by Steve Miller

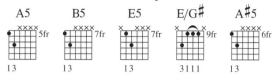

Strum Pattern: 1
Pick Pattern: 5

Intro
Moderately

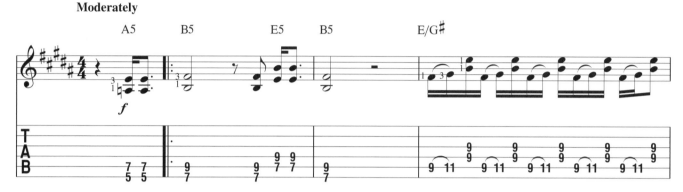

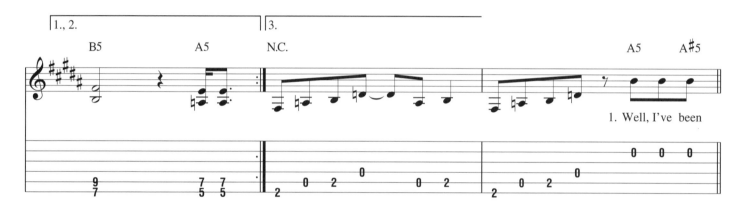

1. Well, I've been

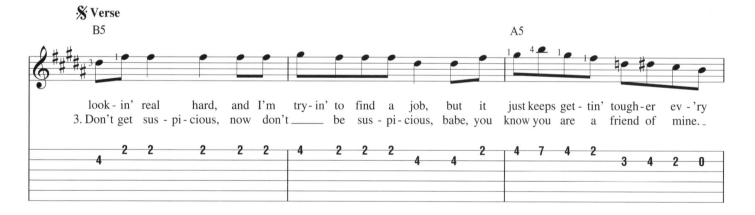

look-in' real hard, and I'm try-in' to find a job, but it just keeps get-tin' tough-er ev-'ry
3. Don't get sus-pi-cious, now don't _____ be sus-pi-cious, babe, you know you are a friend of mine. _____

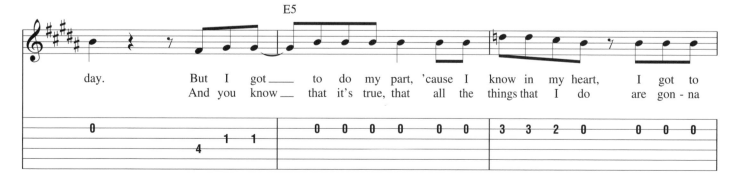

day. But I got _____ to do my part, 'cause I know in my heart, I got to
And you know _____ that it's true, that all the things that I do are gon-na

B5

please my sweet mm, ba - by, yeah, ___   Well, I ain't ___ sup - er - sti - tious, and I
come back to you in your sweet time. ___   I went from Phoe-nix, Ar - i - zo - na, all the

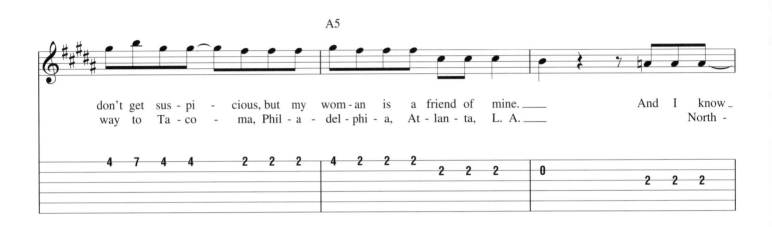

A5

don't get sus - pi - cious, but my wom-an is a friend of mine. ___   And I know ___
way to Ta - co - ma, Phil - a - del - phi - a, At - lan - ta, L. A. ___   North -

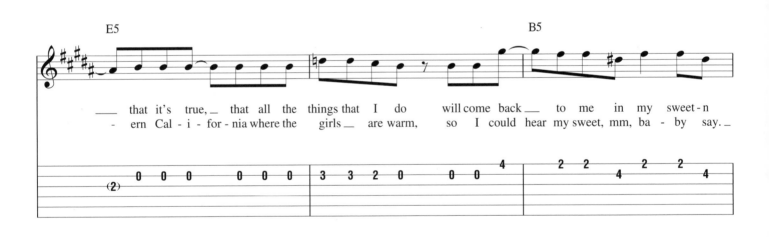

E5   **B5**

___ that it's true, ___ that all the things that I do   will come back ___ to me in my sweet-n
- ern Cal - i - for - nia where the girls ___ are warm,   so I could hear my sweet, mm, ba - by say. ___

To Coda ⊕ **Chorus**

B5

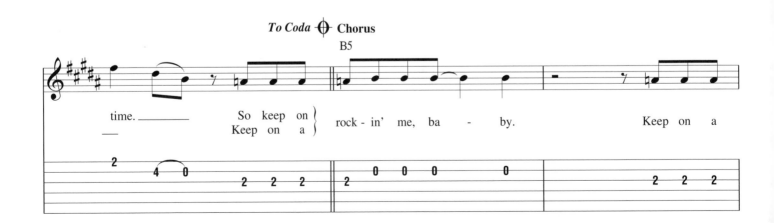

time. ___   So keep on ⎫   rock - in' me, ba - by.   Keep on a
___   Keep on a ⎭

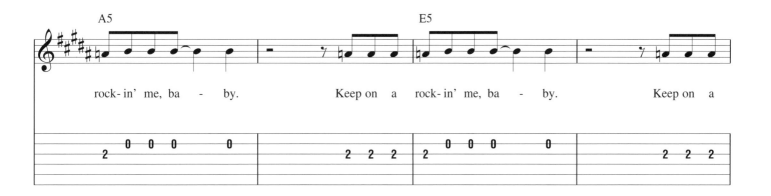

rock-in' me, ba - by. Keep on a rock-in' me, ba - by. Keep on a

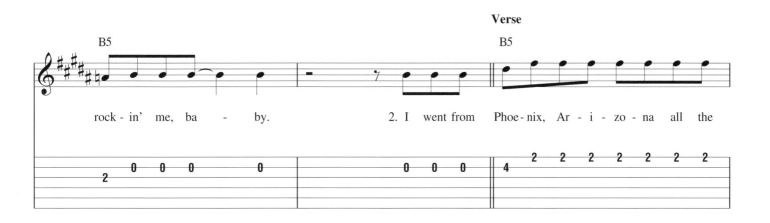

Verse

rock - in' me, ba - by. 2. I went from Phoe-nix, Ar - i - zo - na all the

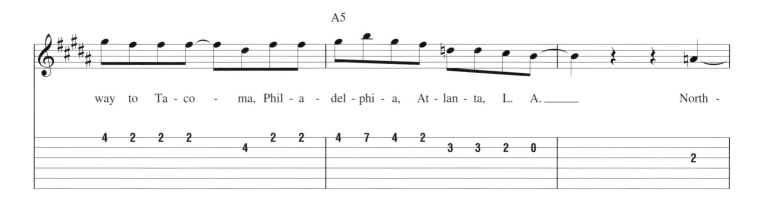

way to Ta - co - ma, Phil - a - del - phi - a, At - lan - ta, L. A. ____ North -

- ern Cal - i - for - nia where the girls are warm, so I can be with my sweet ba - by, yeah.

Chorus

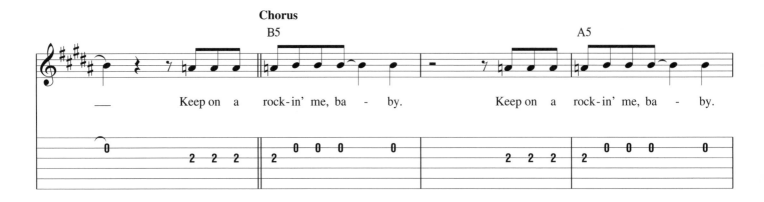

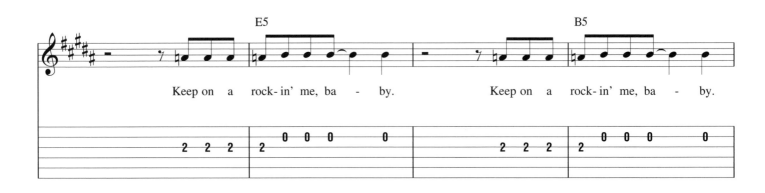

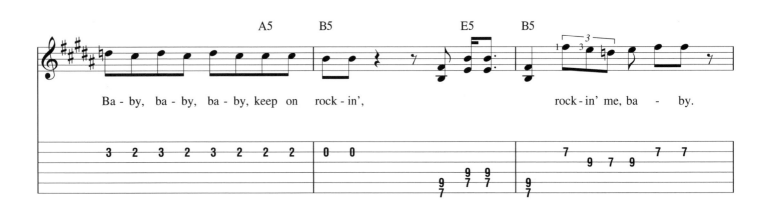

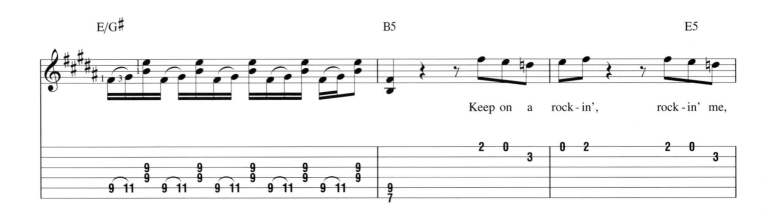

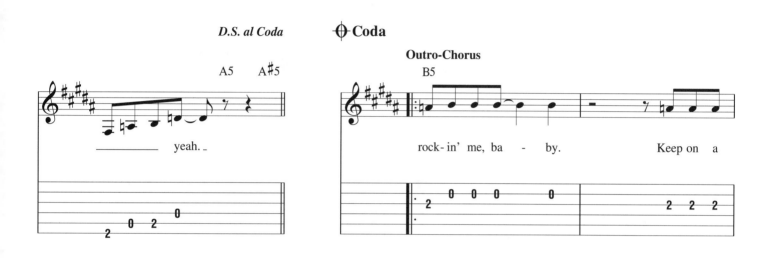

Swingtown

Words and Music by Steve Miller and Chris McCarty

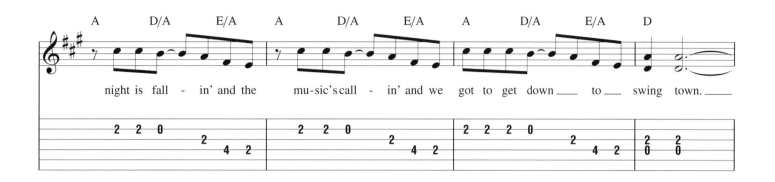

night is fall - in' and the mu-sic's call - in' and we got to get down ___ to ___ swing town. ___

To Coda ✛ **Chorus**

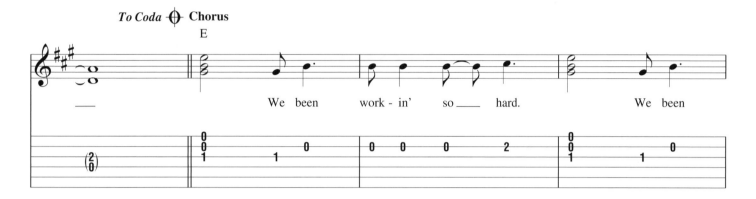

___ We been work - in' so ___ hard. We been

work - in' so ___ hard. Come on, ba - by, come on, ba - by let's dance. _ Did - dy,

D.S. al Coda
(take repeat)

bomp, de, bomp, _ de, bomp. Did - dy bomp, de, bomp, _ de, bomp. Did - dy bomp, de, bomp, _ de, bomp. Oh,

✛ **Coda**

Guitar Solo

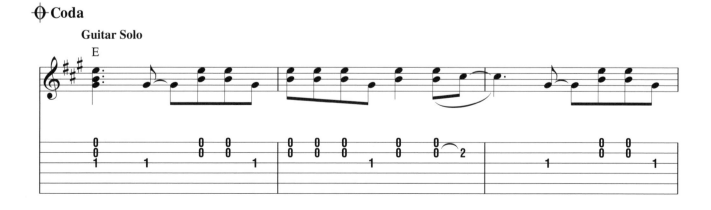

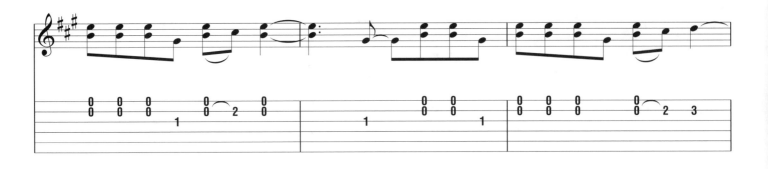

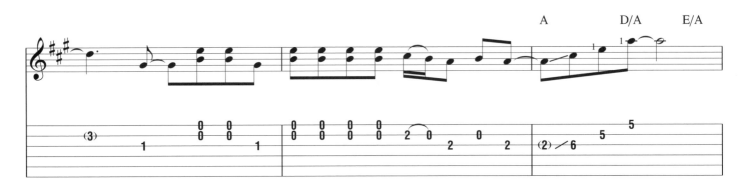

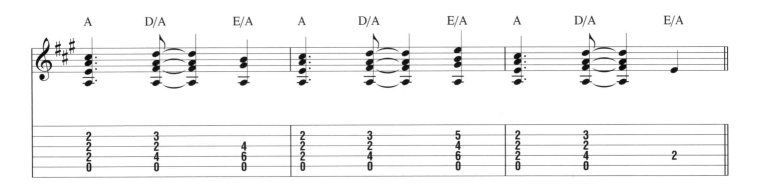

Outro

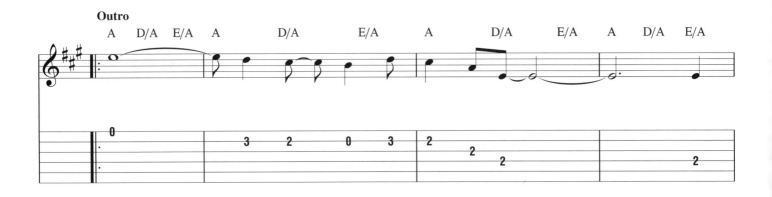

Repeat and fade

Living in the U.S.A.

Words and Music by Steve Miller

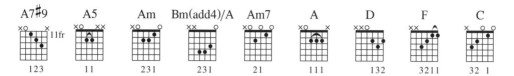

Strum Pattern: 5
Pick Pattern: 6

Intro
Fast

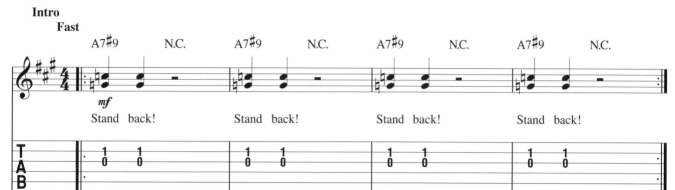

Stand back!   Stand back!   Stand back!   Stand back!

Play 3 times

Chorus

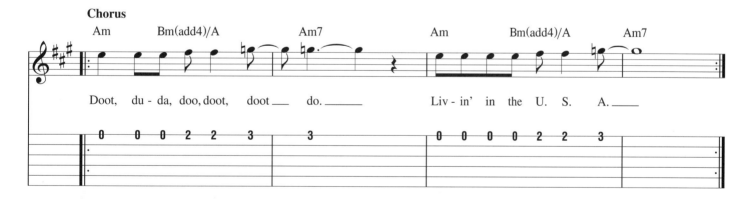

Doot, du - da, doo, doot, doot ___ do. ___ Liv - in' in the U. S. A. ___

Verse

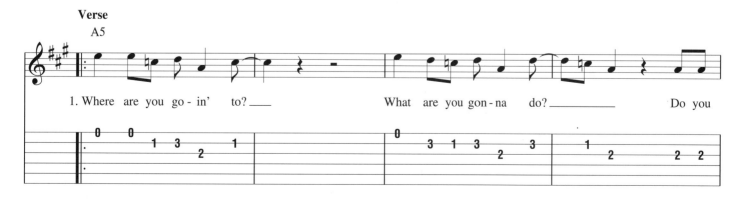

1. Where are you go - in' to? ___ What are you gon - na do? ___ Do you

think that it will be eas - y? _____ You think that it will be pleas -

Pre-Chorus

- in? Hey, ___ hey. Whad'd you say? __ I won't pay. __

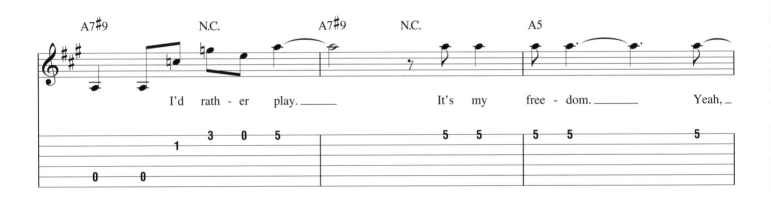

I'd rath - er play. _____ It's my free - dom. _____ Yeah, __

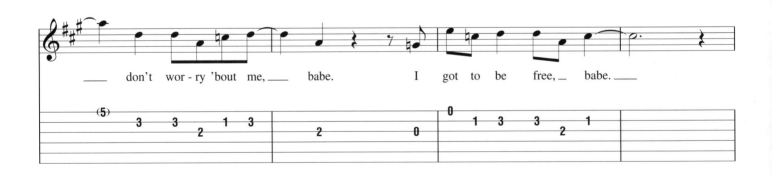

__ don't wor - ry 'bout me, __ babe. I got to be free, _ babe. __

Hey, _____ yeah. _____

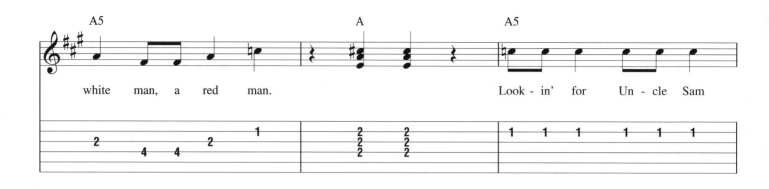

white man, a red man. Look - in' for Un - cle Sam

to give you a help - ing hand. ___ So

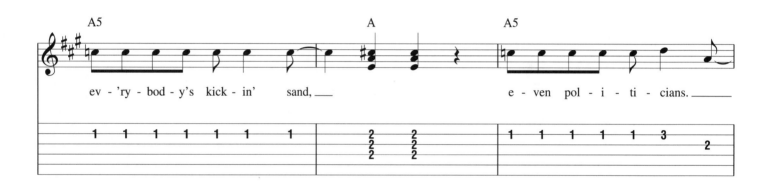

ev - 'ry - bod - y's kick - in' sand, ___ e - ven pol - i - ti - cians. ___

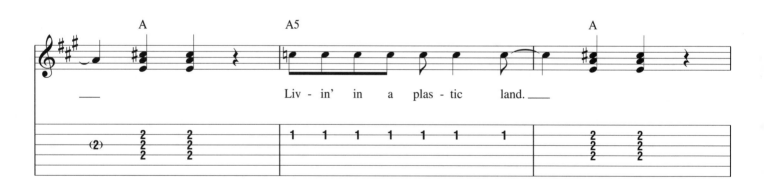

___ Liv - in' in a plas - tic land. ___

Bridge

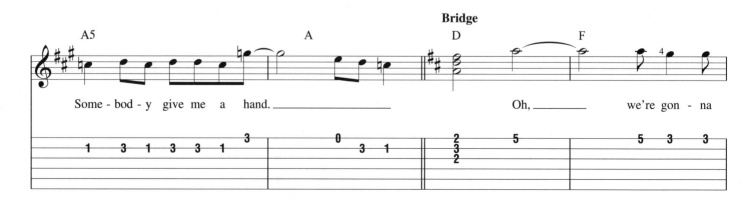

Some - bod - y give me a hand. ___ Oh, ___ we're gon - na

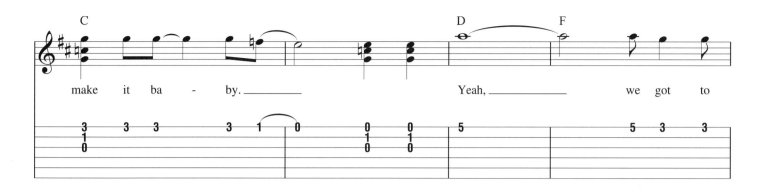

make it ba - by. _____ Yeah, _____ we got to

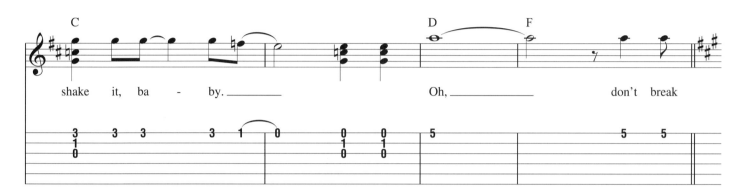

shake it, ba - by. _____ Oh, _____ don't break

Chorus
w/ Voc. ad lib.

it.

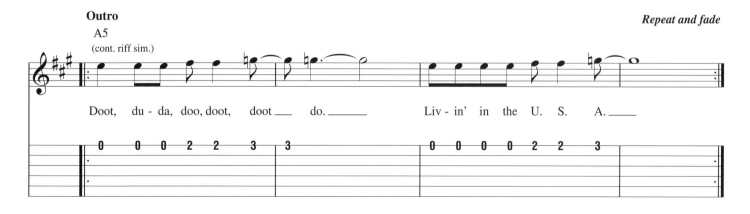

Outro

Repeat and fade

Doot, du - da, doo, doot, doot __ do. _____ Liv - in' in the U. S. A. _____

The Joker

Words and Music by Steve Miller, Eddie Curtis and Ahmet Ertegun

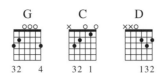

Strum Pattern: 3
Pick Pattern: 2

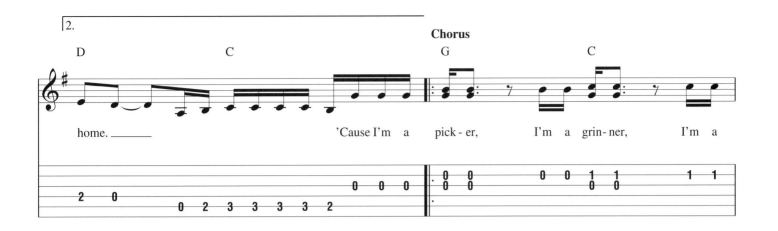

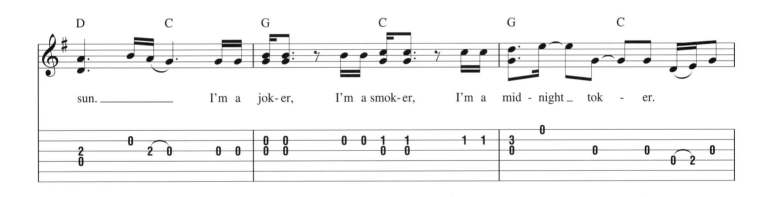

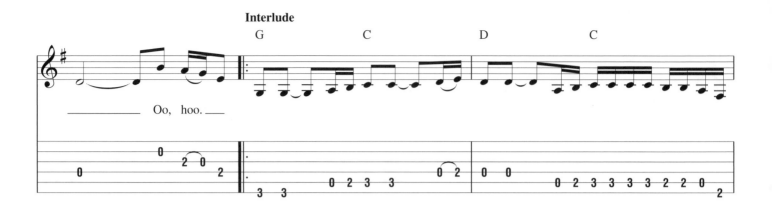

Oo, hoo.

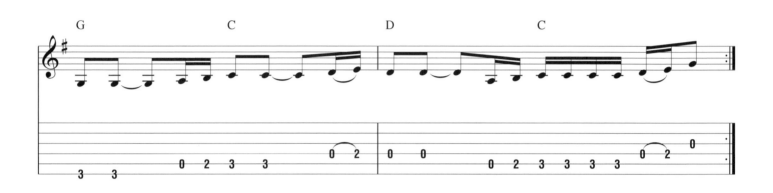

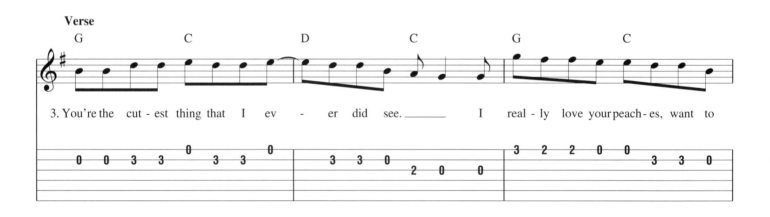

3. You're the cut - est thing that I ev - er did see._____ I real - ly love your peach - es, want to

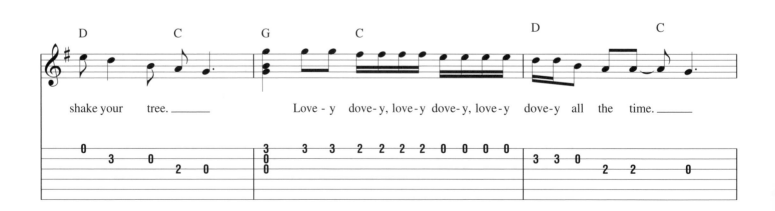

shake your tree._____ Love - y dove - y, love - y dove - y, love - y dove - y all the time._____

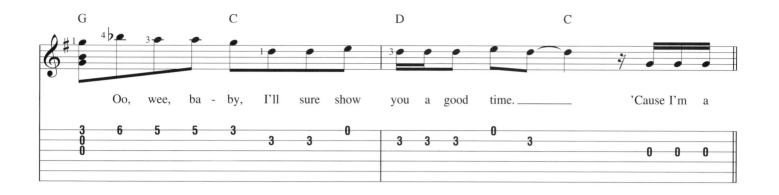

Oo, wee, ba - by, I'll sure show you a good time._____ 'Cause I'm a

Outro-Chorus

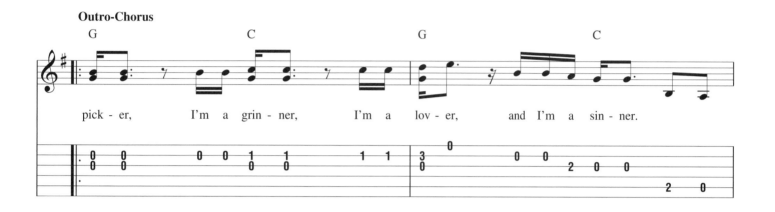

pick - er, I'm a grin - ner, I'm a lov - er, and I'm a sin - ner.

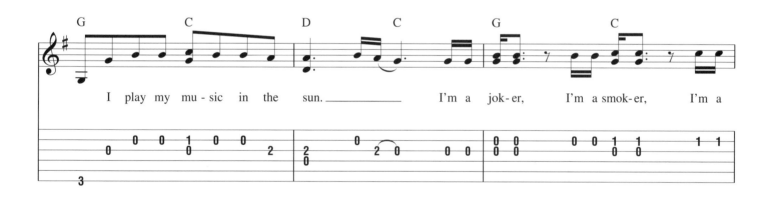

I play my mu - sic in the sun._____ I'm a jok - er, I'm a smok - er, I'm a

Repeat and fade

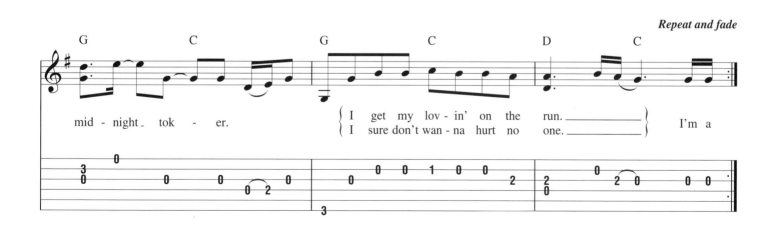

mid - night_ tok - er.

I get my lov - in' on the run._____
I sure don't wan - na hurt no one._____

I'm a

Fly Like an Eagle

Words and Music by Steve Miller

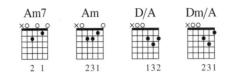

Strum Pattern: 3
Pick Pattern: 4

Intro
Moderately

Tick, tock,_ tick. Doot, doot, do, do.

Verse

Play 4 times

1. Time keeps on slip-pin', slip-pin',

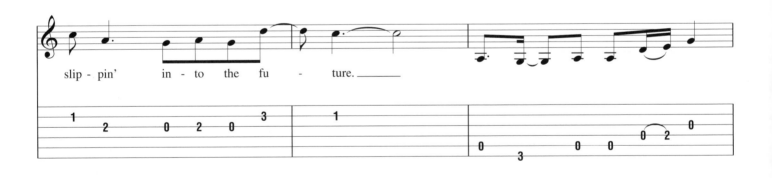

slip-pin'_ in-to the fu - ture. _____

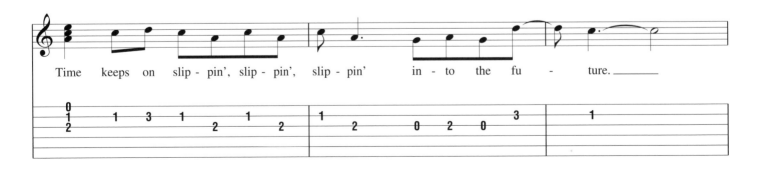

Time keeps on slip-pin', slip-pin', slip-pin' in-to the fu - ture. _____

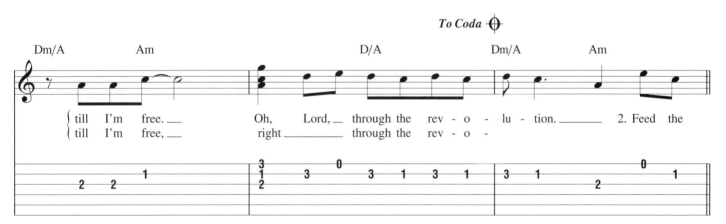

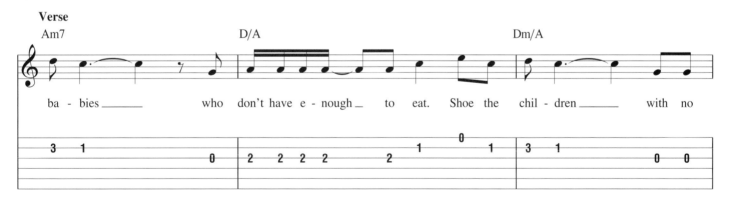

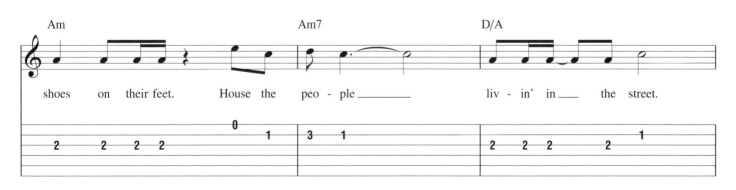

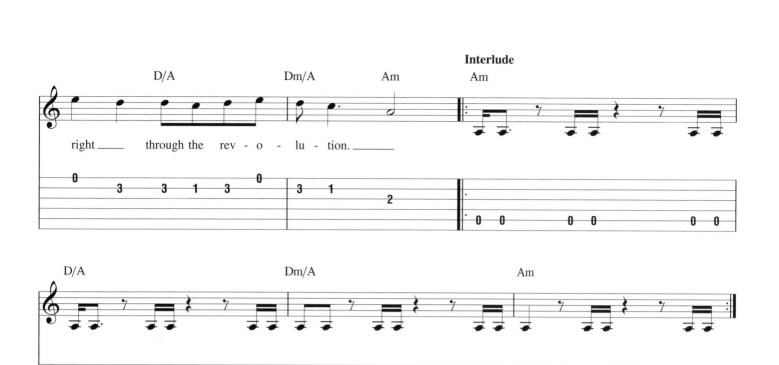

right ____ through the rev - o - lu - tion. ____

Interlude

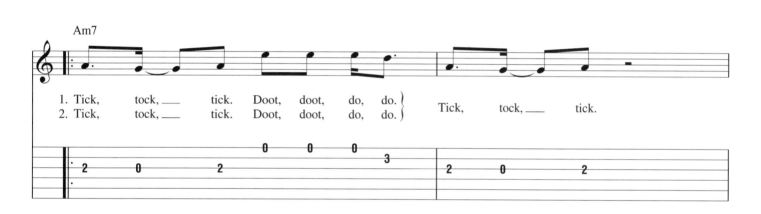

1. Tick, tock, ____ tick. Doot, doot, do, do. }
2. Tick, tock, ____ tick. Doot, doot, do, do. }   Tick, tock, ____ tick.

Outro

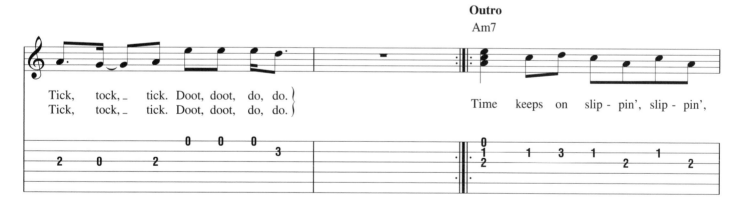

Tick, tock, _ tick. Doot, doot, do, do. }
Tick, tock, _ tick. Doot, doot, do, do. }

Time keeps on slip - pin', slip - pin',

Repeat and fade

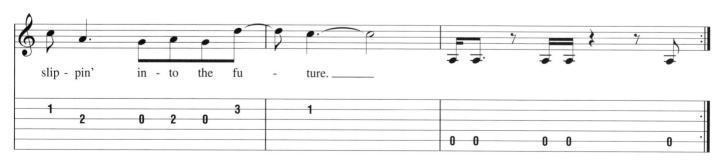

slip - pin' in - to the fu - ture. ____

Jet Airliner

Words and Music by Paul Pena

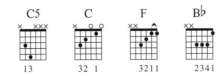

Strum Pattern: 1
Pick Pattern: 6

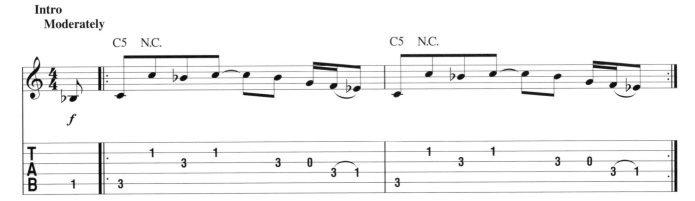

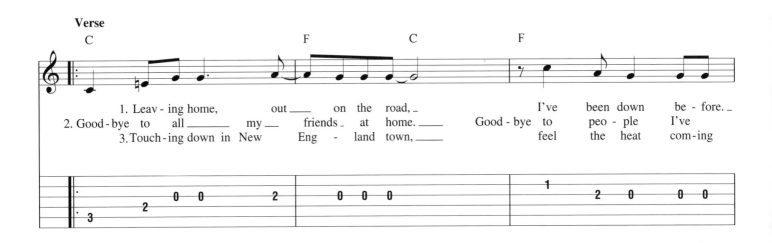

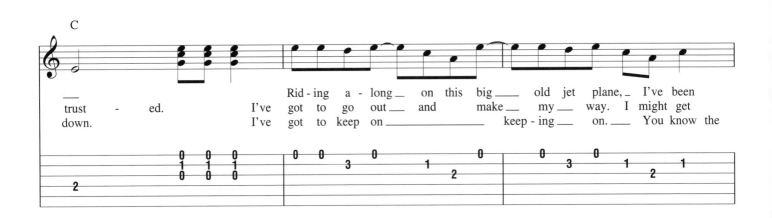

Space Cowboy

Words and Music by Steve Miller and Ben Sidran

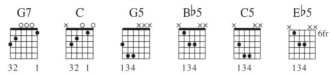

Strum Pattern: 1
Pick Pattern: 3

Intro
Moderately

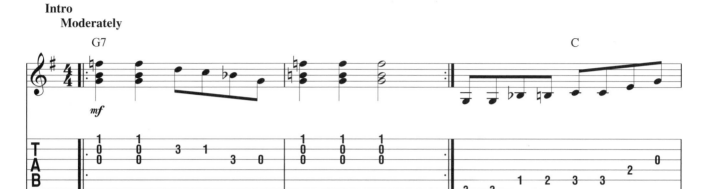

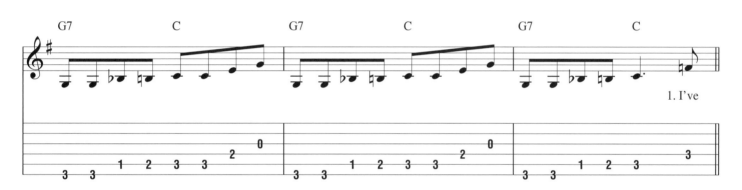

1. I've

Verse

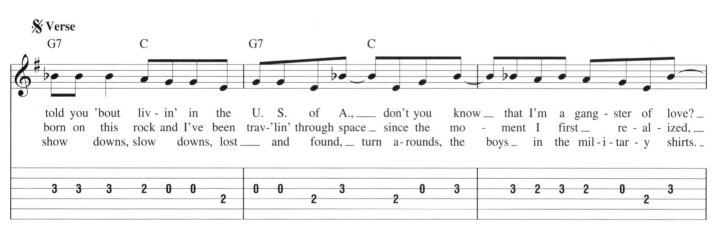

told you 'bout liv-in' in the U. S. of A., don't you know that I'm a gang-ster of love?
born on this rock and I've been trav-'lin' through space since the mo-ment I first re-al-ized,
show downs, slow downs, lost and found, turn a-rounds, the boys in the mil-i-tar-y shirts.

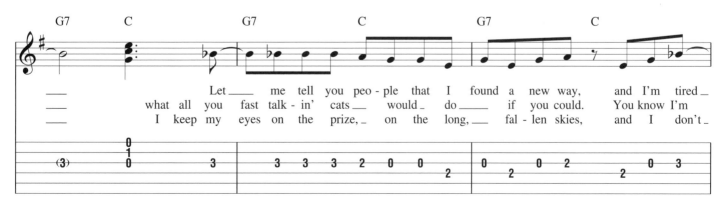

Let me tell you peo-ple that I found a new way, and I'm tired
what all you fast talk-in' cats would do if you could. You know I'm
I keep my eyes on the prize, on the long, fal-len skies, and I don't

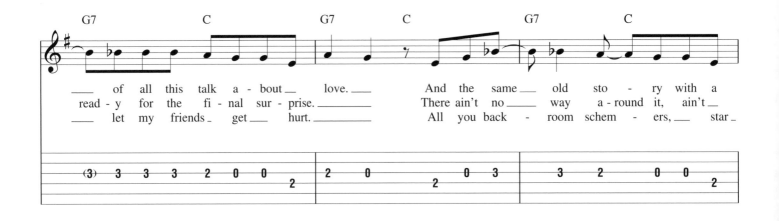

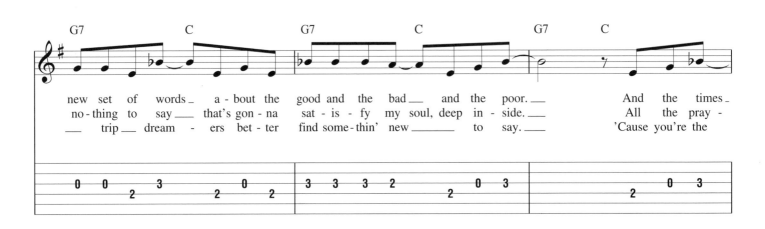

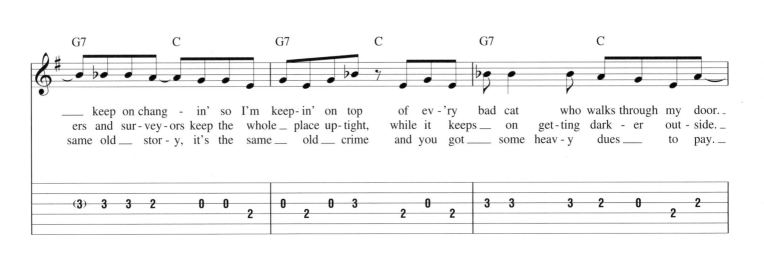

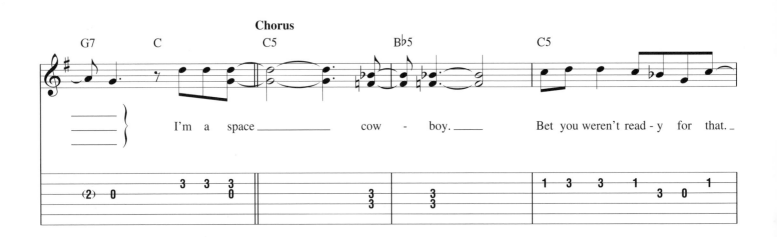

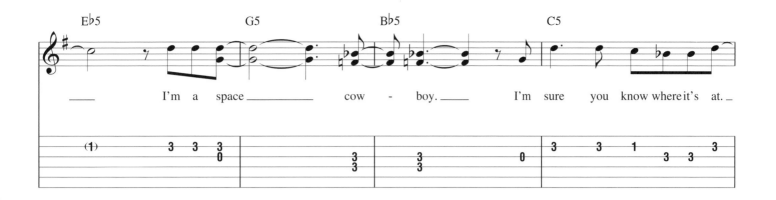

I'm a space _____ cow - boy. ____ I'm sure you know where it's at. __

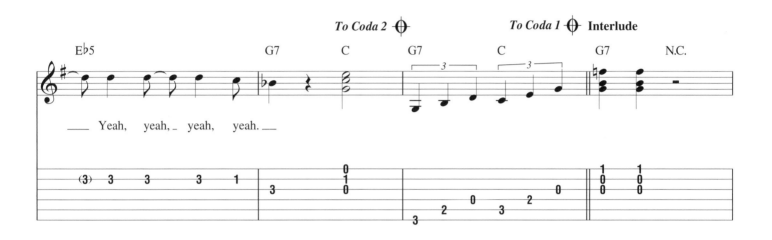

To Coda 2 ⊕   *To Coda 1* ⊕ **Interlude**

__ Yeah, yeah, _ yeah, yeah. __

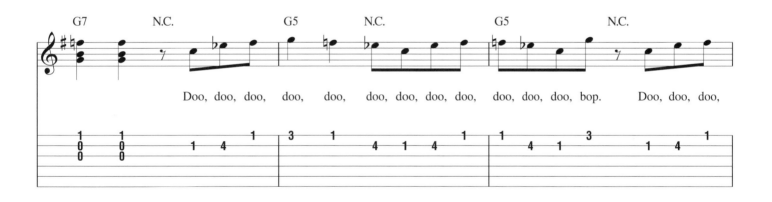

Doo, doo, doo, doo, doo, doo, doo, doo, doo, doo, doo, doo, bop.   Doo, doo, doo,

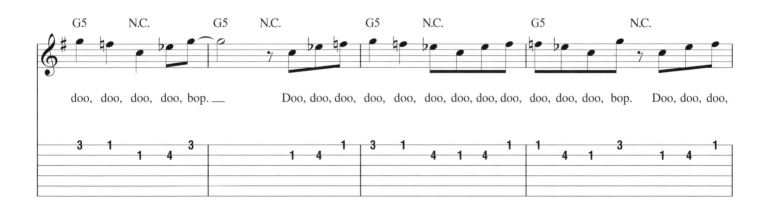

doo, doo, doo, doo, bop. __   Doo, doo, doo, doo, doo, doo, doo, doo, doo, doo, doo, doo, bop.   Doo, doo, doo,

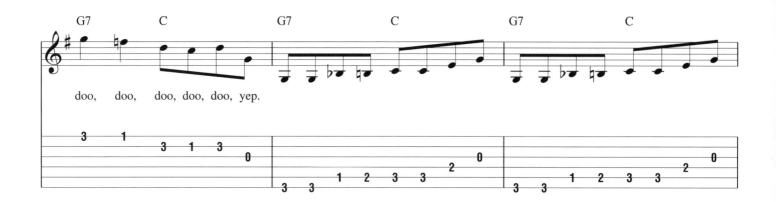

doo,   doo,   doo, doo, doo, yep.

D.S. al Coda 1   ⊕ **Coda 1**

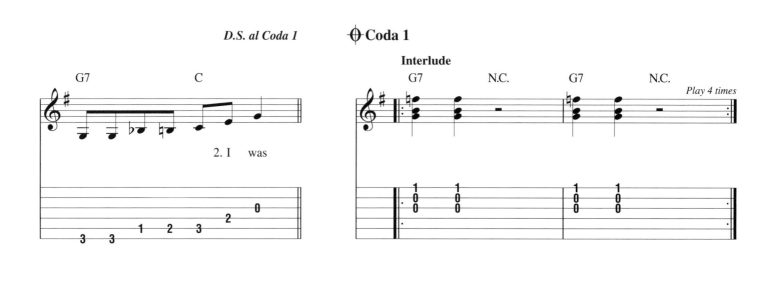

2. I   was

Interlude

Play 4 times

Guitar Solo

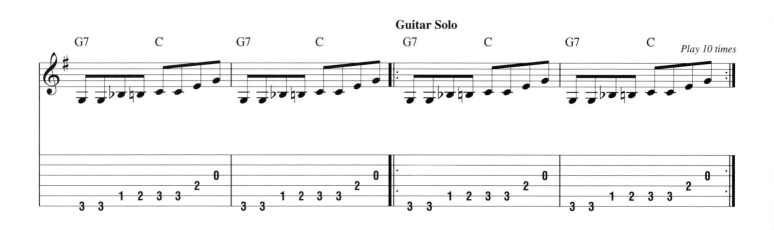

Play 10 times

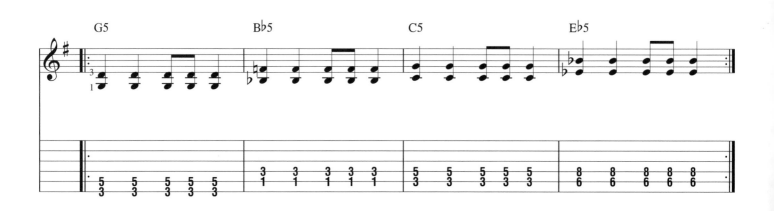

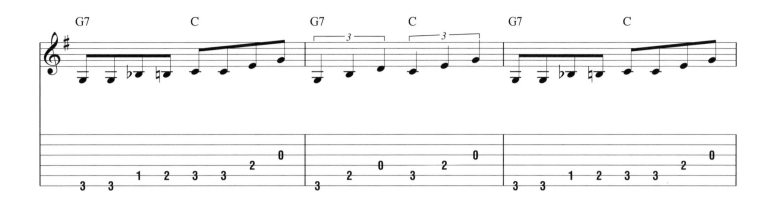

D.S. al Coda 2

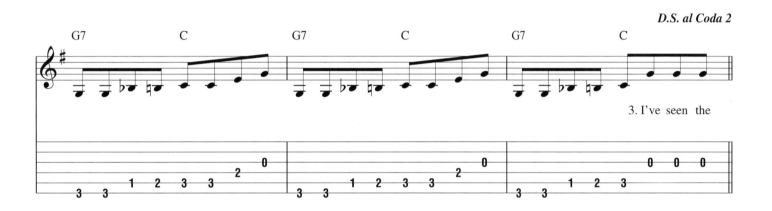

3. I've seen the

 Coda 2

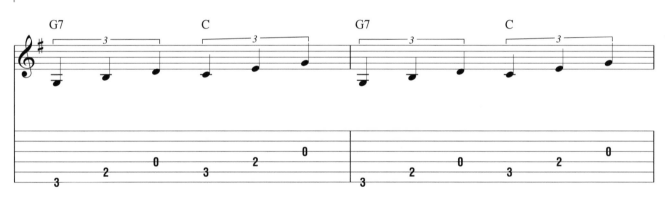

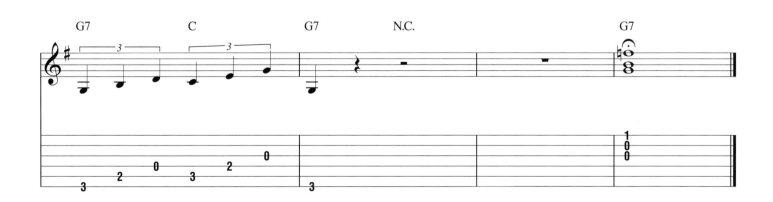

Jungle Love

Words and Music by Lonnie Turner and Greg Douglas

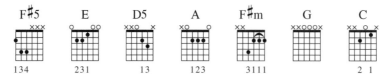

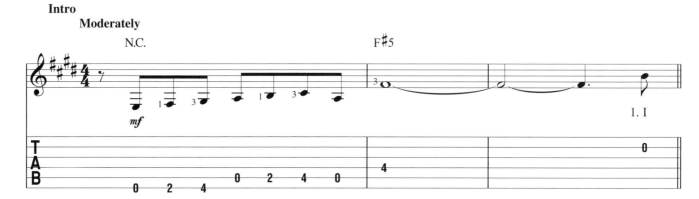

Strum Pattern: 2
Pick Pattern: 6

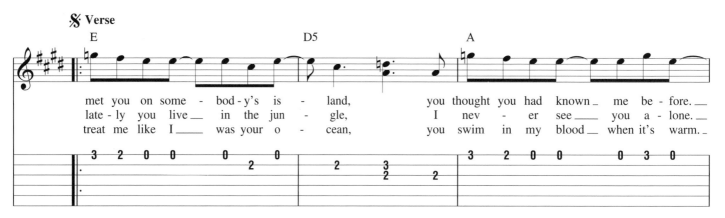

met you on some-bod-y's is-land, you thought you had known me be-fore.
late-ly you live in the jun-gle, I nev-er see you a-lone.
treat me like I was your o-cean, you swim in my blood when it's warm.

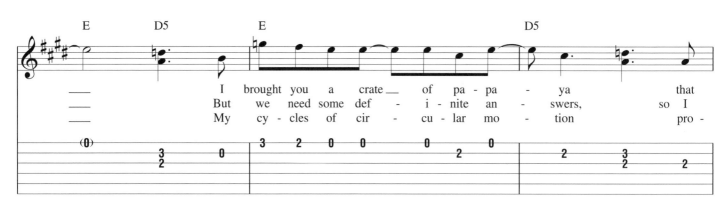

I brought you a crate of pa-pa-ya that
But we need some def-i-nite an-swers, so I
My cy-cles of cir-cu-lar mo-tion pro-

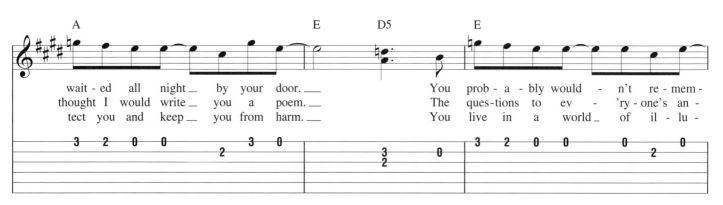

wait-ed all night by your door. You prob-a-bly would-n't re-mem-
thought I would write you a poem. The ques-tions to ev-'ry-one's an-
tect you and keep you from harm. You live in a world of il-lu-

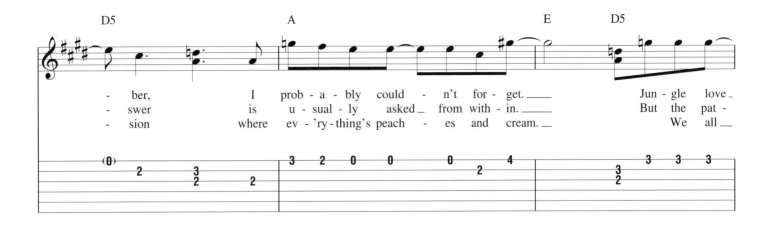

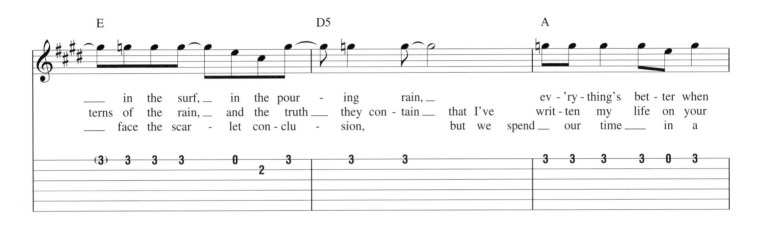

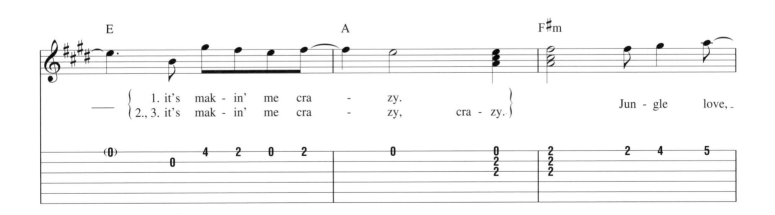

it's driv - in' me mad,_____ it's mak - in' me cra - zy._____

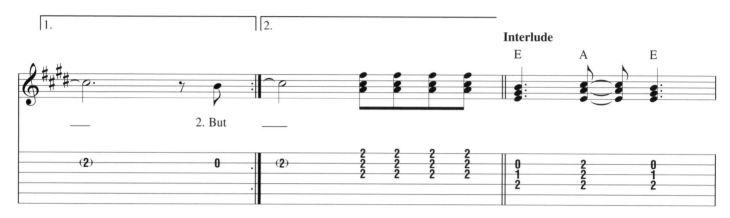

Interlude

2. But_____

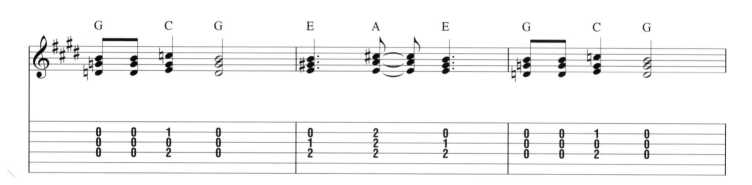

To Coda ⊕

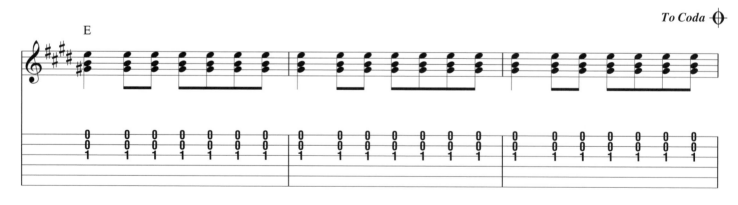

D.S. al Coda
(take 2nd ending)

3. You

⊕ **Coda**

N.C.

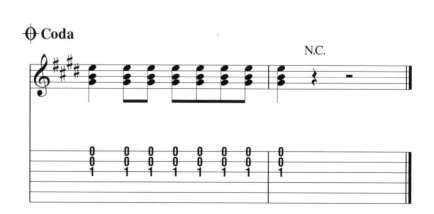

Serenade From the Stars

Words and Music by Steve Miller and Chris McCarty

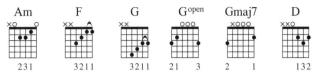

Strum Pattern: 1
Pick Pattern: 1

Intro
Moderate Rock

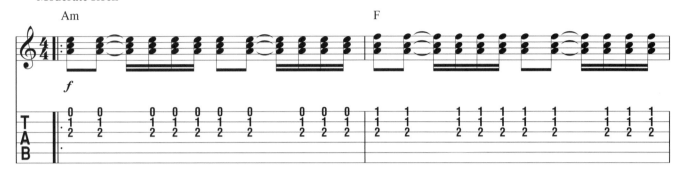

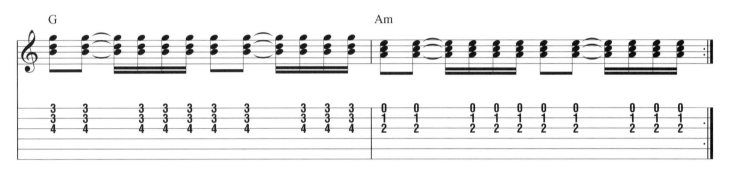

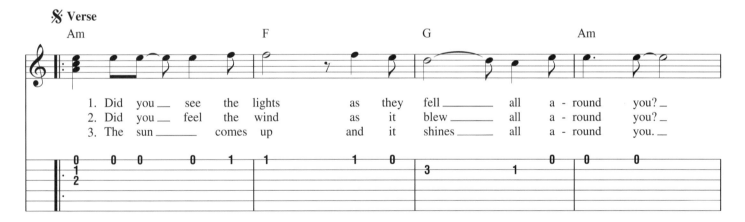

1. Did you ___ see the lights as they fell _____ all a-round you? ___
2. Did you ___ feel the wind as it blew _____ all a-round you? ___
3. The sun _____ comes up and it shines _____ all a-round you. ___

To Coda

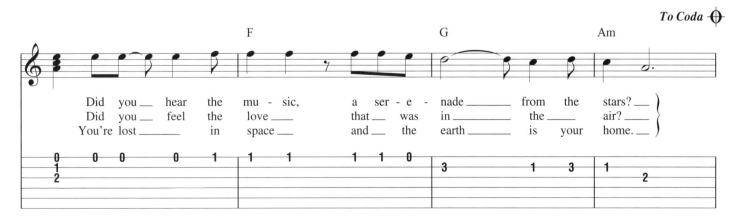

Did you ___ hear the mu-sic, a ser-e-nade _____ from the stars? ___
Did you ___ feel the love ___ that ___ was in the air? ___
You're lost _____ in space ___ and ___ the earth _____ is your home. ___

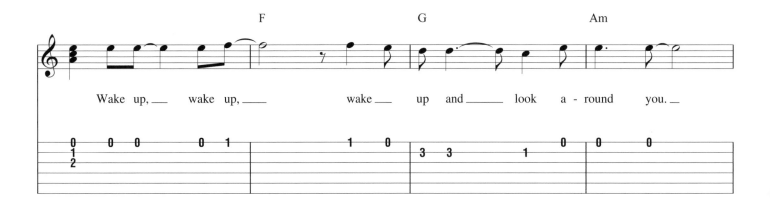

Wake up, ___ wake up, ___ wake ___ up and ___ look a - round you. ___

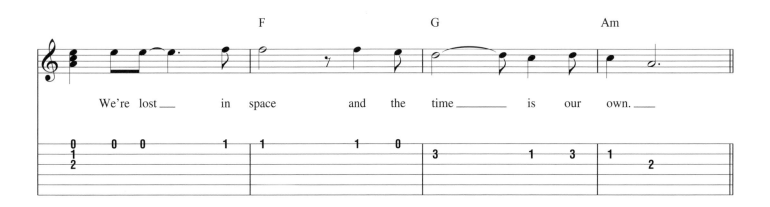

We're lost ___ in space and the time ___ is our own. ___

Interlude

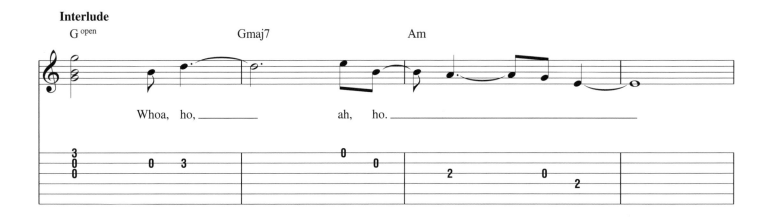

Whoa, ho, _____ ah, ho. _____

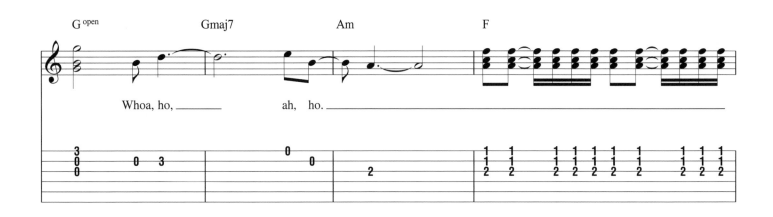

Whoa, ho, _____ ah, ho. _____

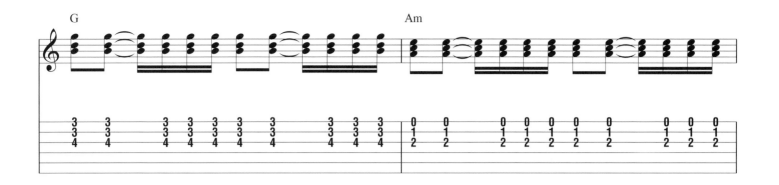

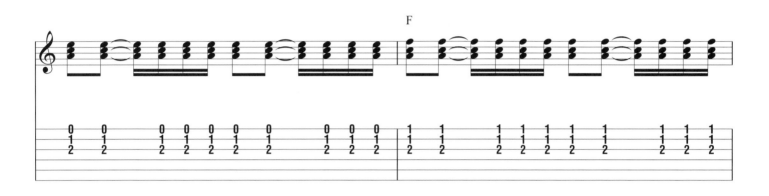

2nd time, D.S. al Coda

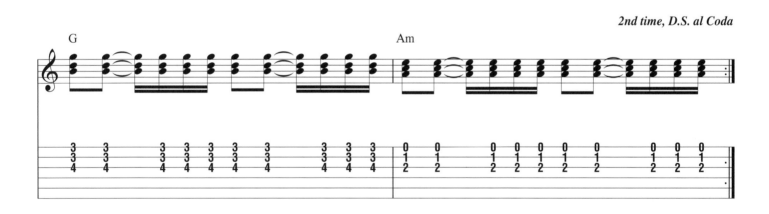

✛ **Coda**

Outro

Repeat and fade

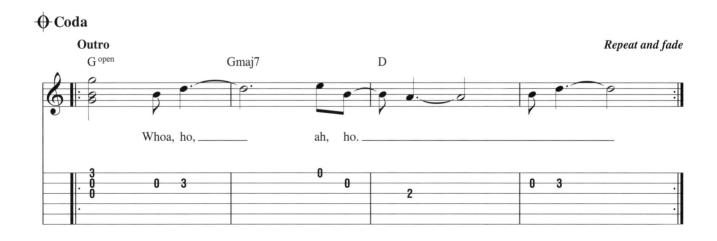

Whoa, ho, _____ ah, ho. _____

47

Cry Cry Cry

Words and Music by Steve Miller

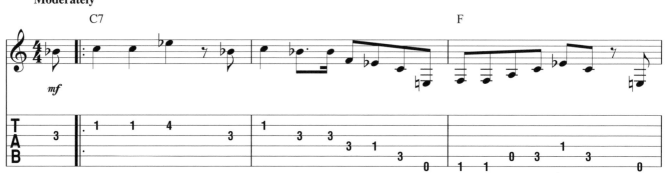

Strum Pattern: 1
Pick Pattern: 3

Intro
Moderately

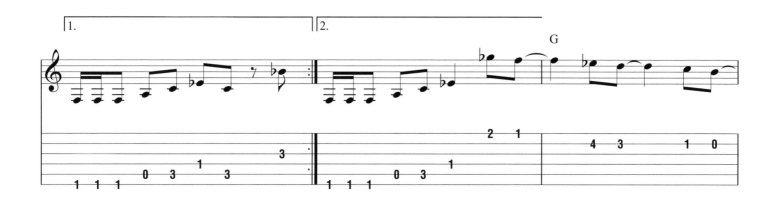

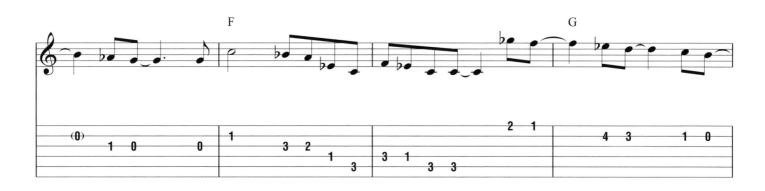

1. I'm gon - na

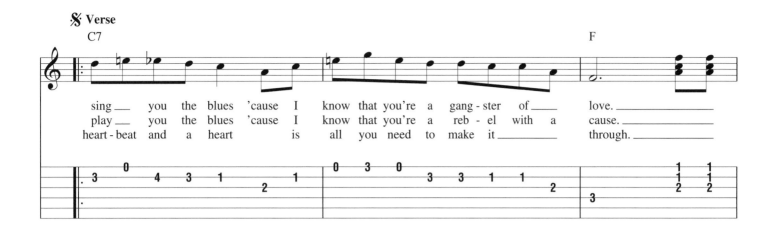

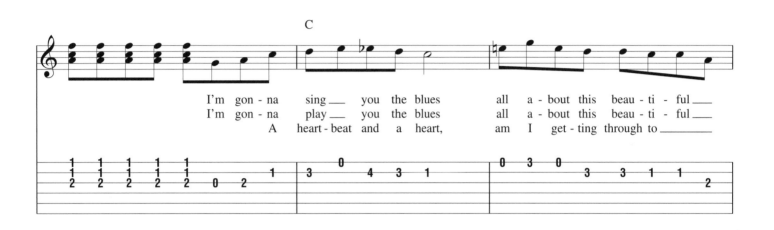

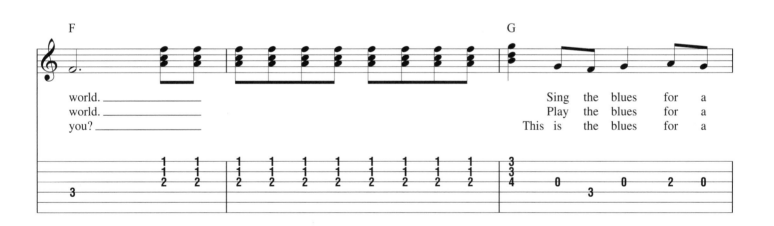

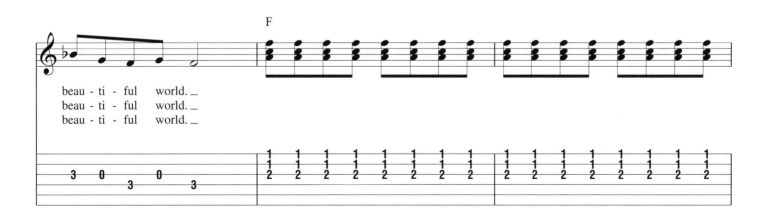

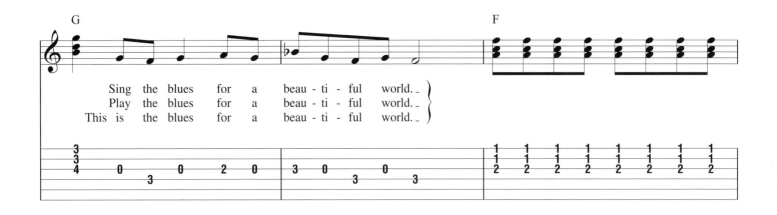

Sing the blues for a beau - ti - ful world. _
Play the blues for a beau - ti - ful world. _
This is the blues for a beau - ti - ful world. _

Chorus

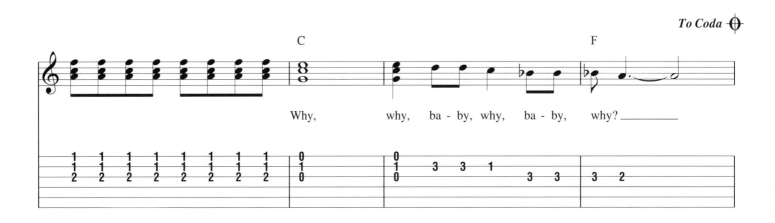

Cry, cry, ba - by, cry, ba - by, cry. _____

To Coda ⊕

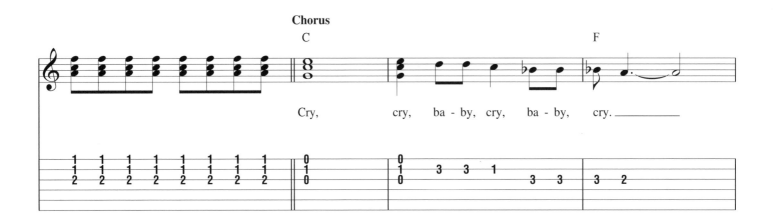

Why, why, ba - by, why, ba - by, why? _____

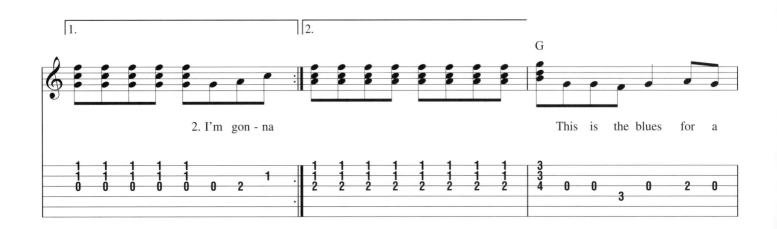

2. I'm gon - na

This is the blues for a

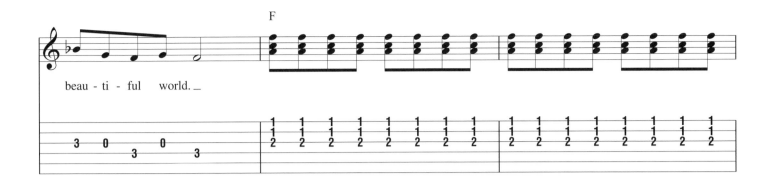

beau - ti - ful world. __

D.S. al Coda

G   F

This is the blues for a beau - ti - ful world. __

3. A

⊕ Coda

Outro-Chorus

C   F

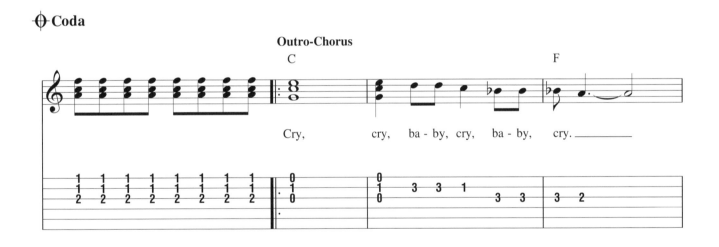

Cry,   cry, ba - by, cry, ba - by, cry. _____

Repeat and fade

C   F

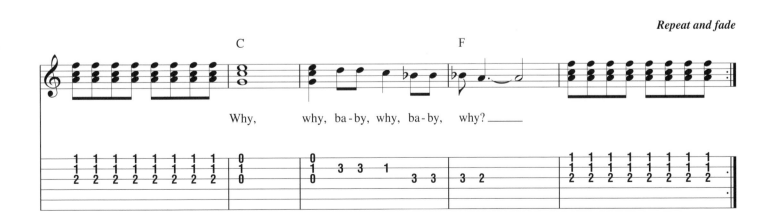

Why,   why, ba - by, why, ba - by, why? _____

Shu Ba Da Du Ma Ma Ma Ma

Words and Music by Steve Miller

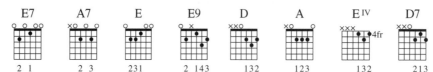

Strum Pattern: 1
Pick Pattern: 3

Intro
Moderately slow

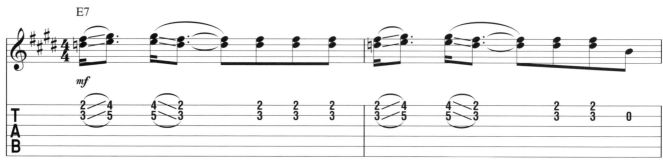

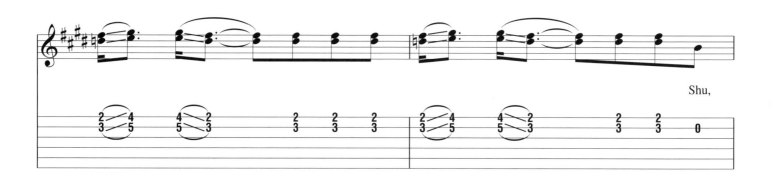

Shu,

ba, da, du, ma,___ ma, ma, ma. Shu, ba, da, du, ma,___ ma, ma. Shu

ba, da, du, ma,___ ma, ma, ma. Shu, ba, da, du, ma,___ ma, ma. Yeah.___

Verse

E7

1., 3. Come on, ba-by, let's   skip a - way. _   You

2. Come on, ba-by, now don't be too slow. _   You

know I'm in   a   hur-ry.   I wan-na leave right a - way. _

know I'm in   a   hur-ry.   I real-ly do want to go. _

Don't make sense   if it   ain't   the   real   thing.

First you're   up   and   then you're   down. _

Noth-in' but the real   thing makes _   my heart sing. _____ }

Cra - zy liv-in'   in this _   old   town. _____ }

Yeah. _   Shu,

Chorus

ba, da, du, ma,___ ma, ma, ma. Shu, ba, da, du, ma,___ ma, ma. Shu,

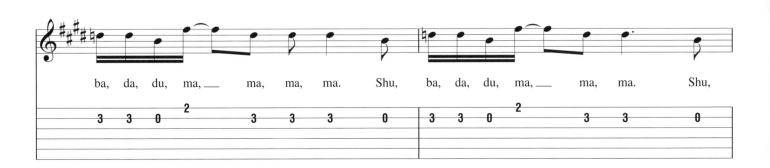

ba, da, du, ma,___ ma, ma, ma. Shu, ba, da, du, ma,___ ma, ma. Shu,

ba, da, du, ma,___ ma, ma, ma. Shu, ba, da, du, ma,___ ma, ma. Shu,

To Coda

ba, da, du, ma,___ ma, ma, ma. Shu, ba, da, du, ma,___ ma, ma. Yeah._____

Interlude

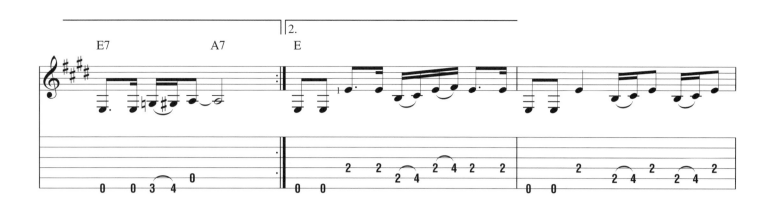

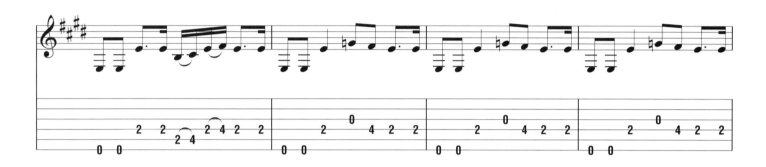

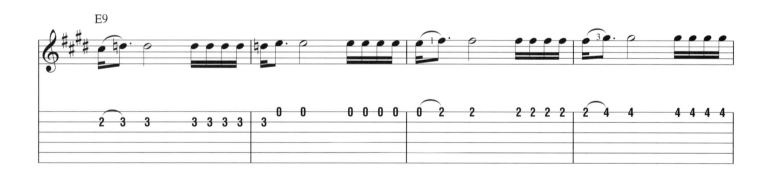

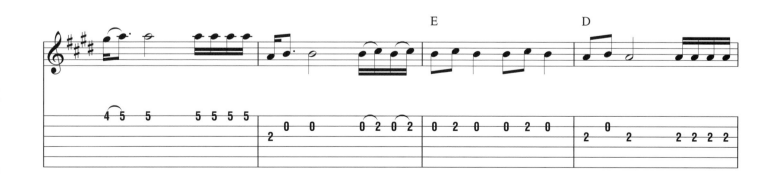

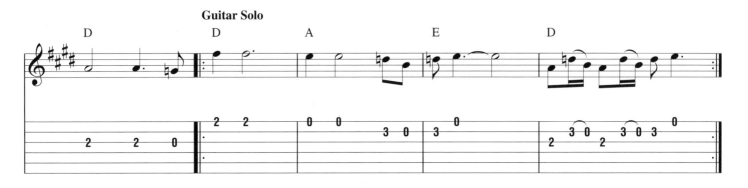

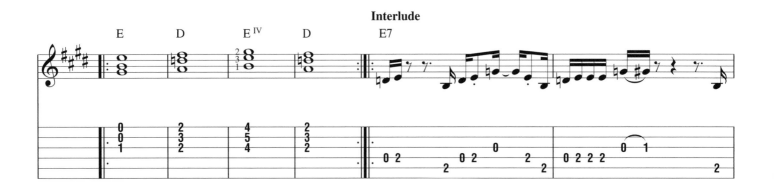

2nd time, D.S. al Coda

$\oplus$ **Coda**

Outro

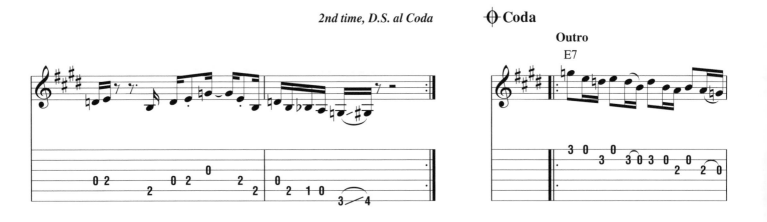

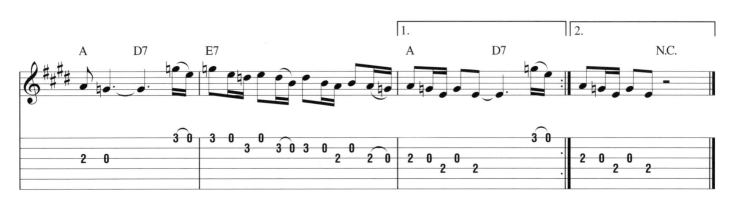

Wide River

Words and Music by Steve Miller and Chris McCarty

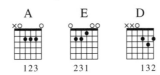

Strum Pattern: 1, 2
Pick Pattern: 1

Intro
Moderately

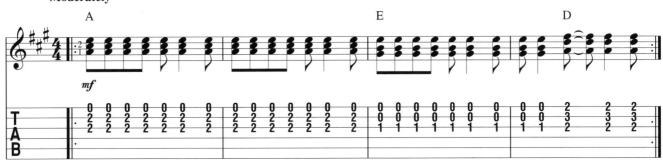

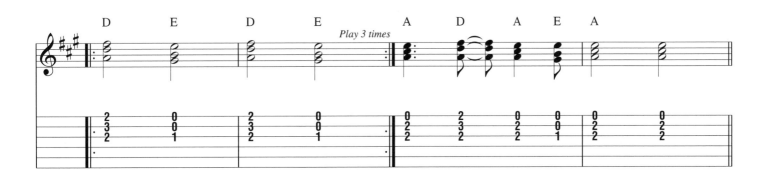

Verse

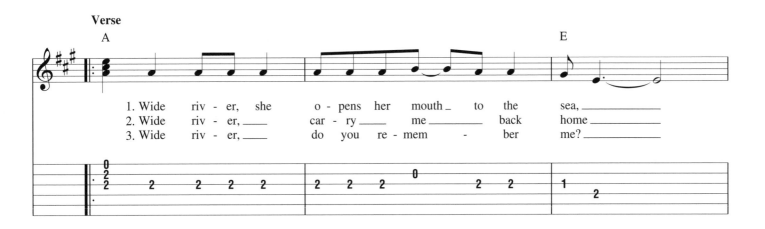

1. Wide riv-er, she o-pens her mouth to the sea,
2. Wide riv-er, car-ry me back home
3. Wide riv-er, do you re-mem - ber me?

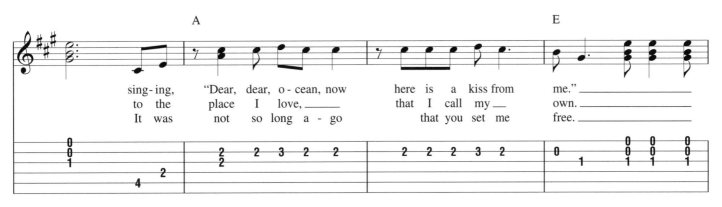

sing-ing, "Dear, dear, o-cean, now here is a kiss from me."
to the place I love, that I call my own.
It was not so long a-go that you set me free.

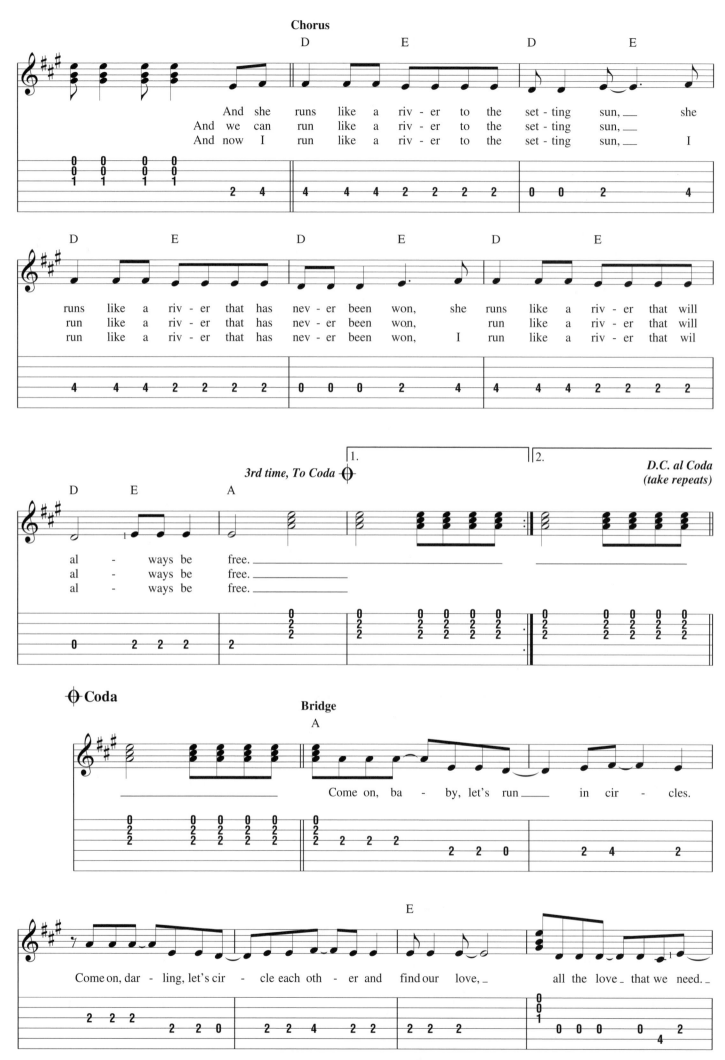

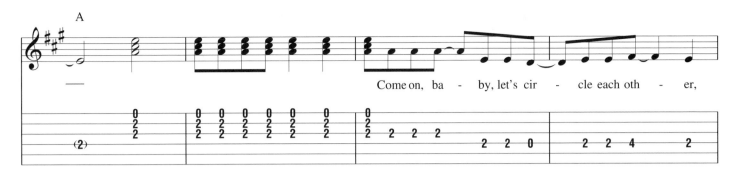

Come on, ba - by, let's cir - cle each oth - er,

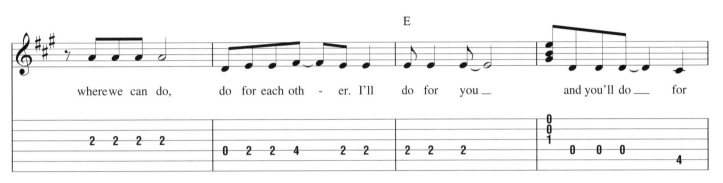

where we can do, do for each oth - er. I'll do for you ___ and you'll do ___ for

Chorus

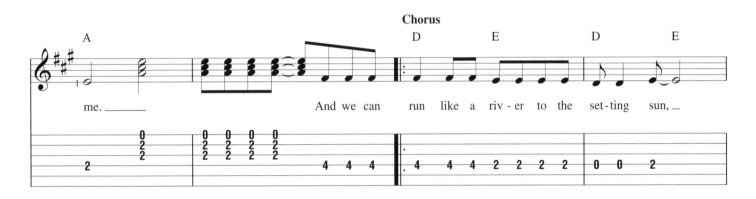

me. ___ And we can run like a riv - er to the set - ting sun, ___

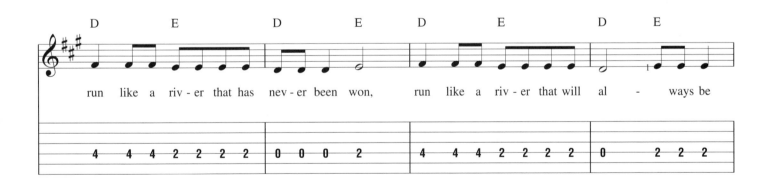

run like a riv - er that has nev - er been won, run like a riv - er that will al - ways be

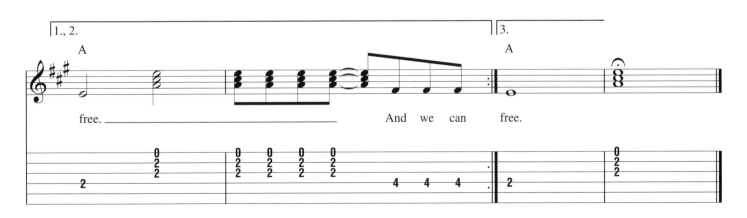

free. ___ And we can free.

Wild Mountain Honey

Words and Music by Steve McCarty

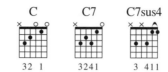

Strum Pattern: 1
Pick Pattern: 3

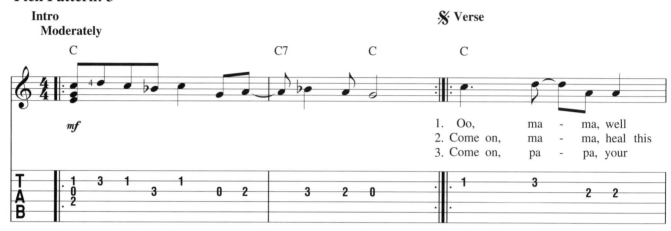

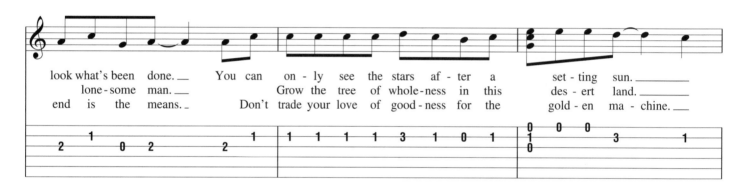

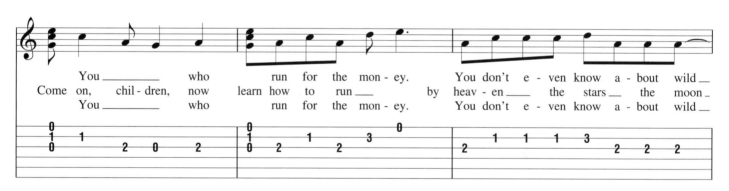

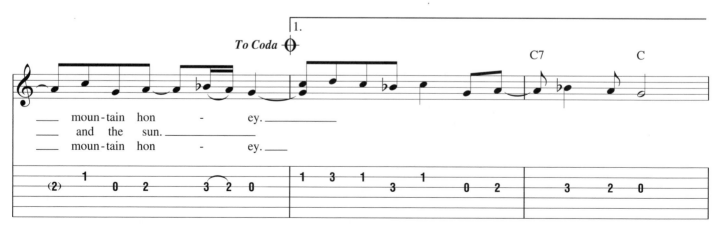

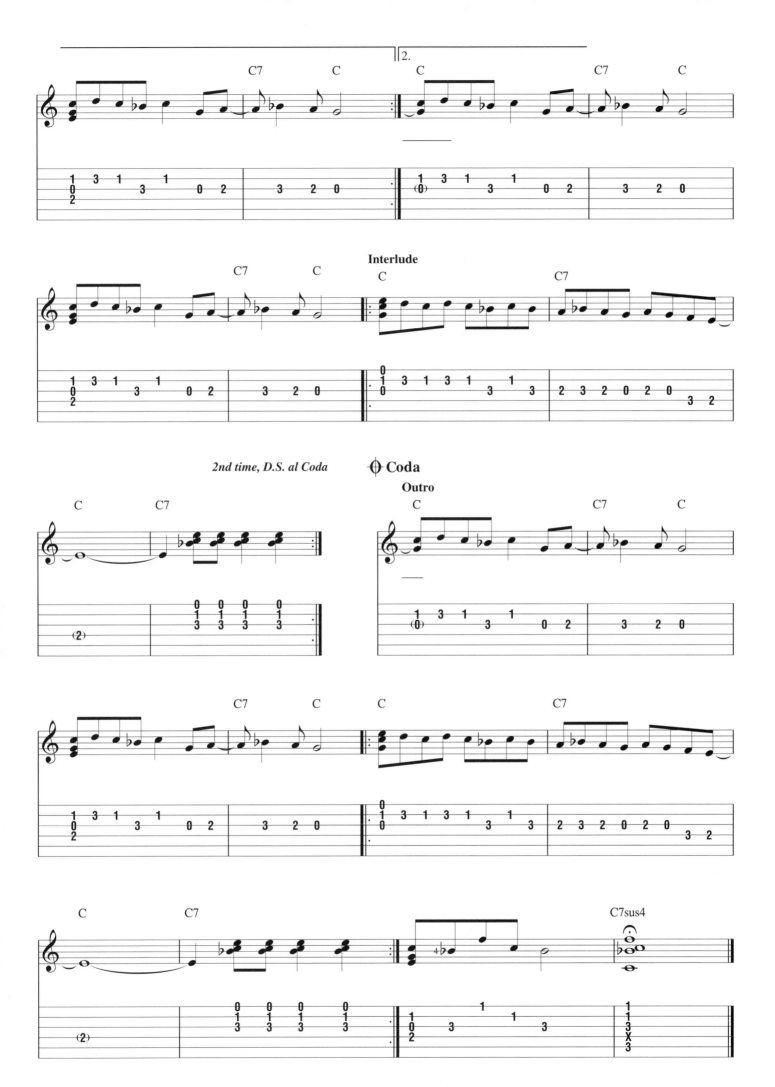

The Stake

Words and Music by David Denny

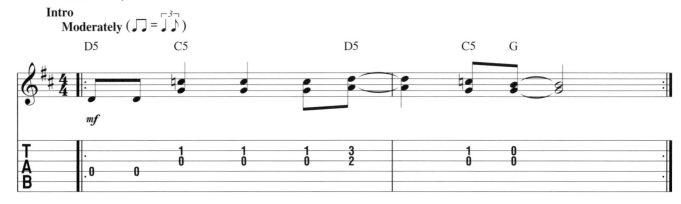

Strum Pattern: 1, 2
Pick Pattern: 3, 4

Intro
Moderately

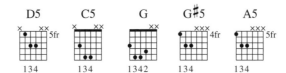

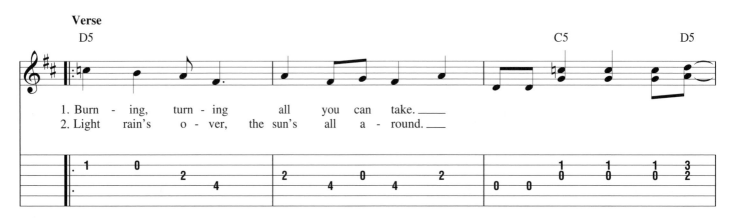

Verse

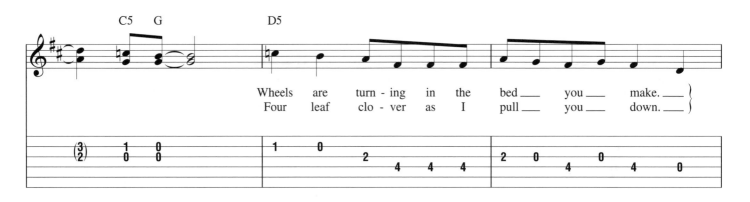

1. Burn - ing, turn - ing all you can take. ____
2. Light rain's o - ver, the sun's all a - round. ____

Wheels are turn - ing in the bed ____ you ____ make. ____
Four leaf clo - ver as I pull ____ you ____ down. ____

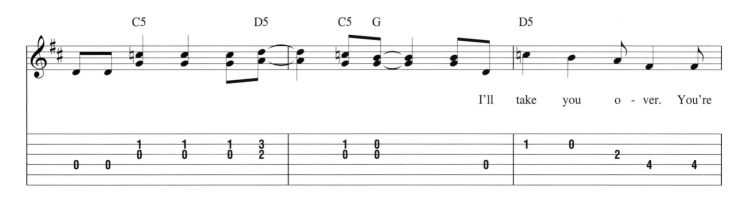

I'll take you o - ver. You're

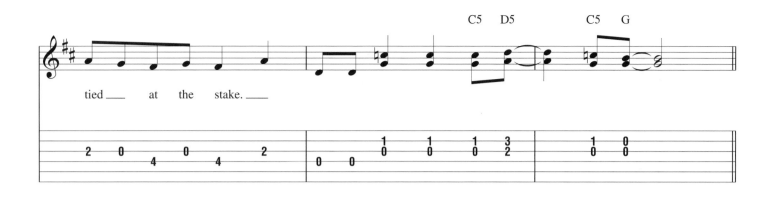

tied ___ at the stake. ___

Chorus

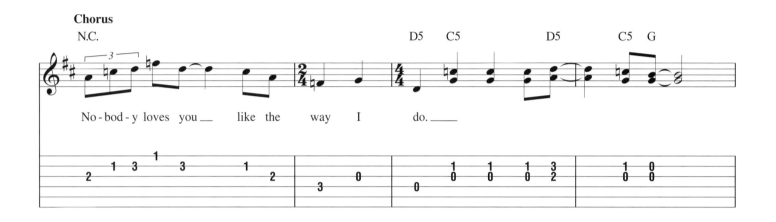

No - bod - y loves you ___ like the way I do. ___

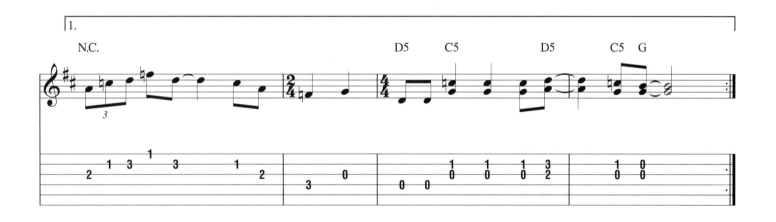

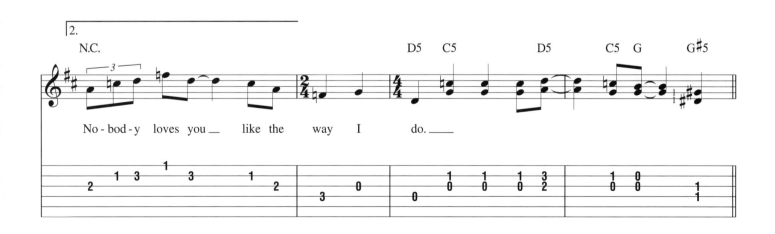

No - bod - y loves you ___ like the way I do. ___

Interlude

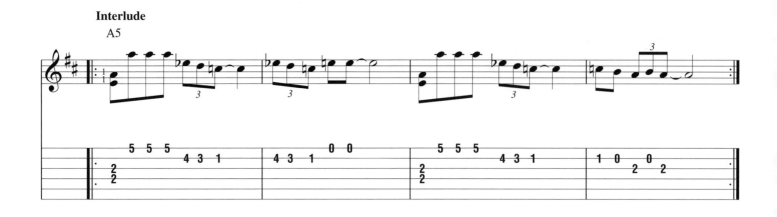

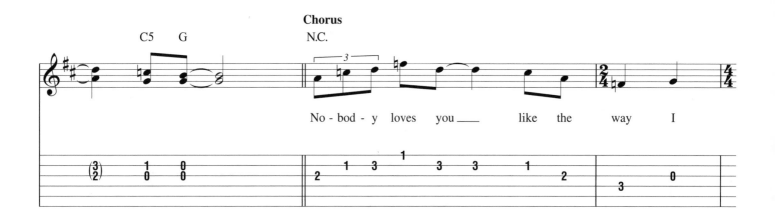

Chorus

No - bod - y loves you____ like the way I

Outro

Repeat and fade

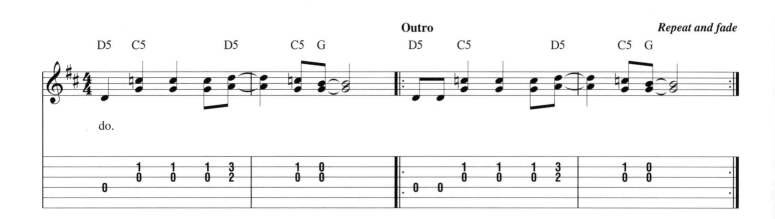

do.

My Dark Hour

Words and Music by Steve Miller and Paul Ramone

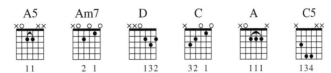

Strum Pattern: 1
Pick Pattern: 3

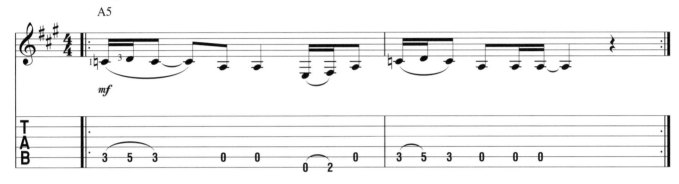

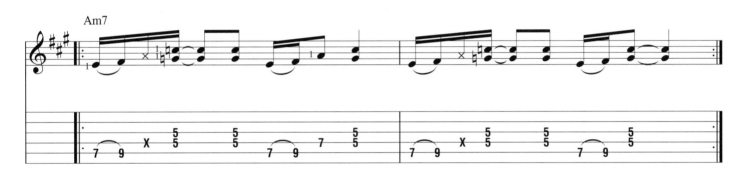

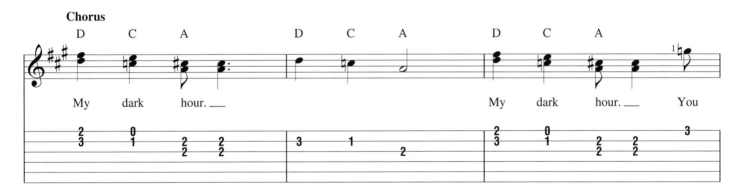

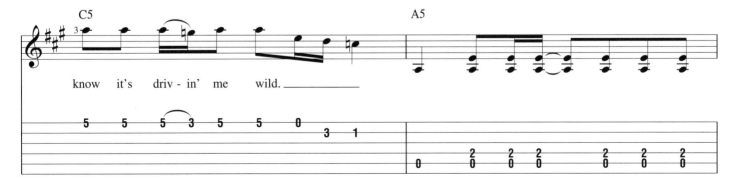

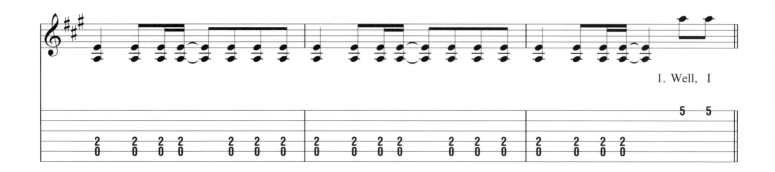

1. Well, I

Verse

| A | D | A | D | A | D |

went to see the doc - tor, and I had my for - tune read. And you know this doc - tor told me,
went to see the doc - tor, just to have my for - tune read. Well, well, well, the doc - tor told me,

C5

Am7

Whispered: "Son, you better stay in bed."
Whispered: "Son, you better stay in bed."

Who's that com - in' down that road? _
Say, do you think these cit - ies will fall, __

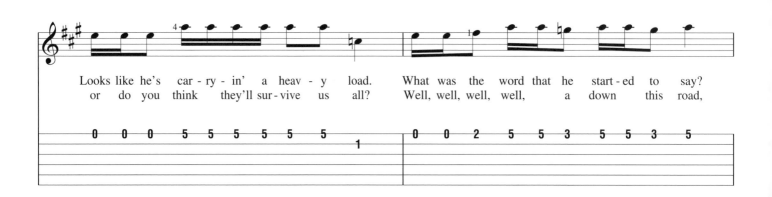

Looks like he's car - ry - in' a heav - y load. What was the word that he start - ed to say?
or do you think they'll sur - vive us all? Well, well, well, well, a down this road,

Chorus

Wan - na come with me, on my way?
won't you help me car - ry my load?

My dark hour. _ Moth - er Na - ture's child.

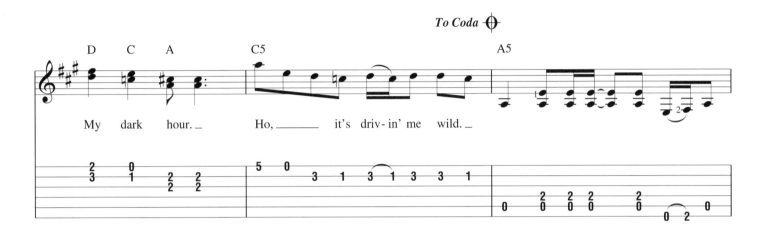

To Coda

My dark hour. _ Ho, _____ it's driv - in' me wild. _

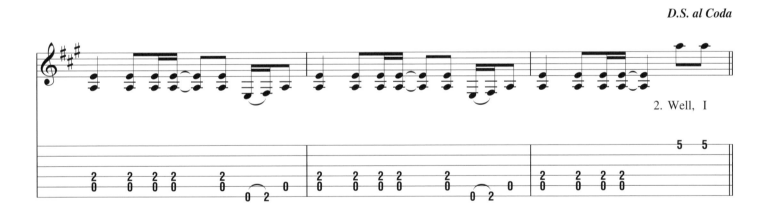

D.S. al Coda

2. Well, I

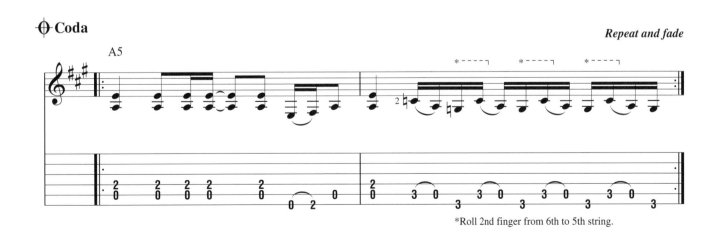

Coda

Repeat and fade

*Roll 2nd finger from 6th to 5th string.

Who Do You Love

Words and Music by Steve Miller and Tim Davis

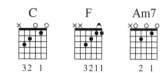

Strum Pattern: 1
Pick Pattern: 3

Intro
Moderately

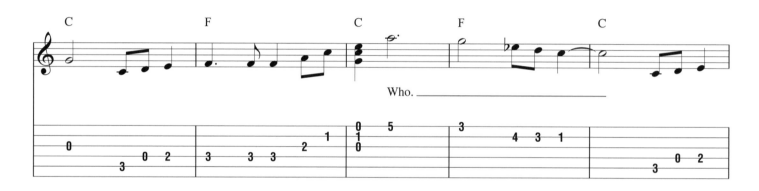

Who. _____

Verse

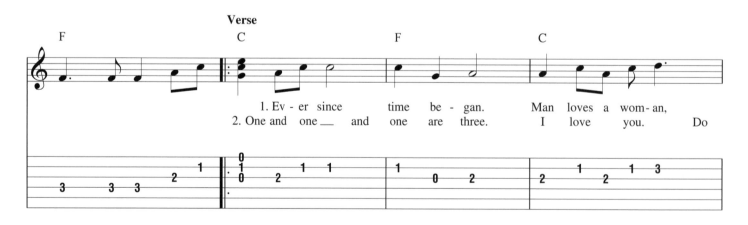

1. Ev - er since time be - gan. Man loves a wom- an,
2. One and one __ and one are three. I love you. Do

wom-an loves a man. This is the way it was meant to be __ through the pa -
you love me? This is the place, now is the time, _____

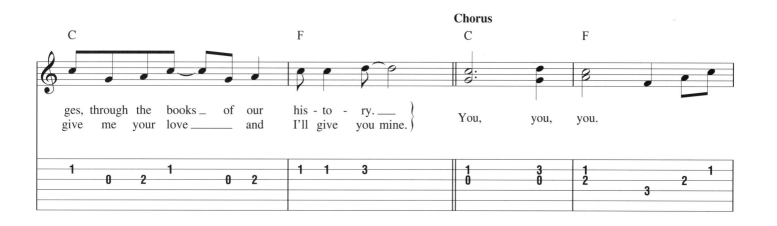

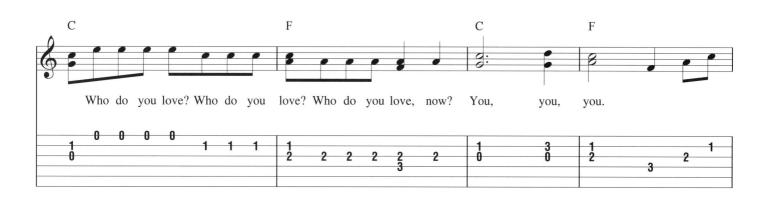

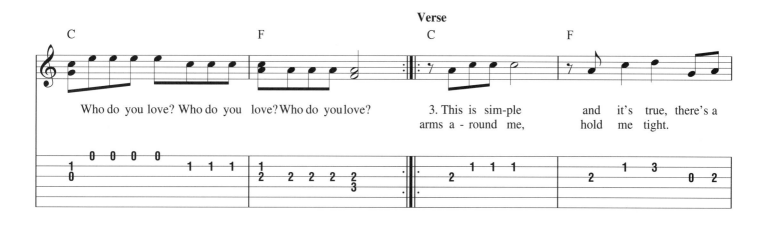

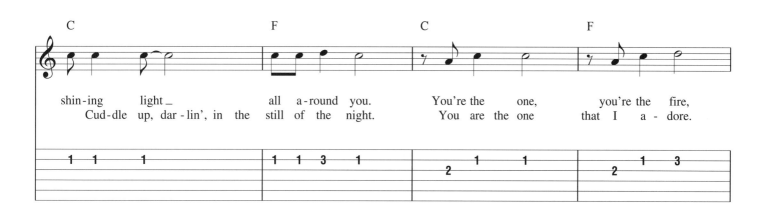

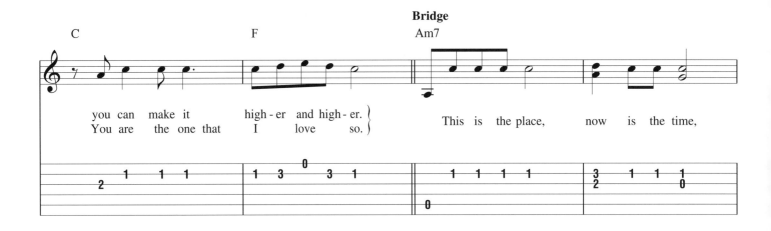

you can make it high-er and high-er.
You are the one that I love so.

This is the place, now is the time,

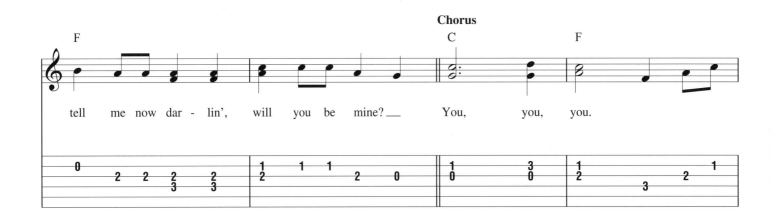

tell me now dar-lin', will you be mine?___ You, you, you.

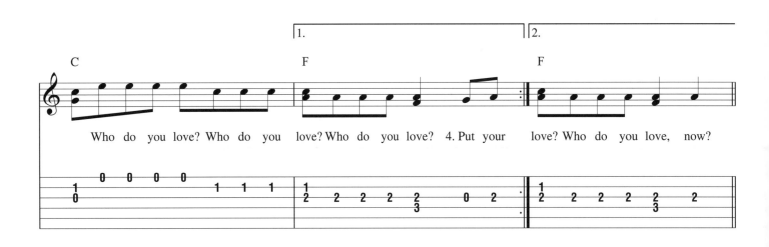

Who do you love? Who do you love? Who do you love? 4. Put your love? Who do you love, now?

Outro-Chorus

Repeat and fade

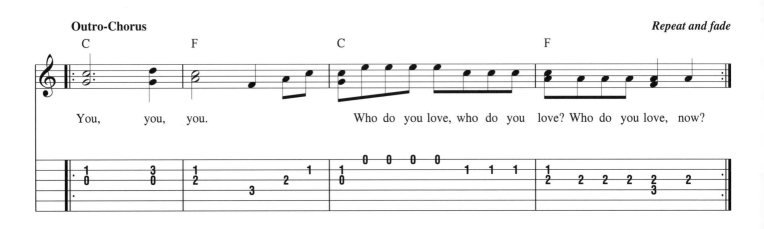

You, you, you. Who do you love, who do you love? Who do you love, now?

I Want to Make the World Turn Around

Words and Music by Steve Miller

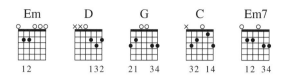

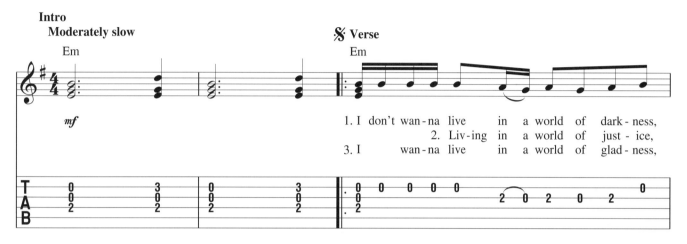

Strum Pattern: 3
Pick Pattern: 6

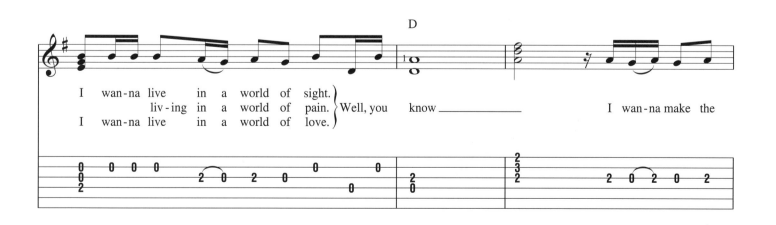

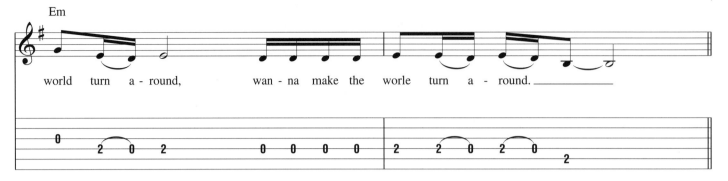

world turn a - round, wan - na make the worle turn a - round. _____

1.

Interlude

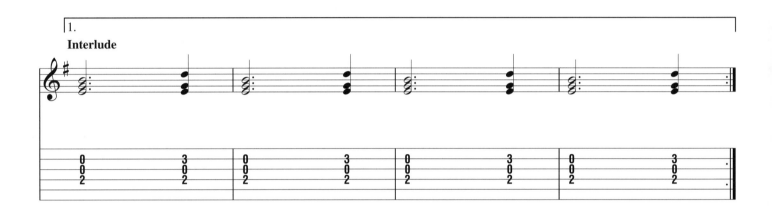

2.

Bridge

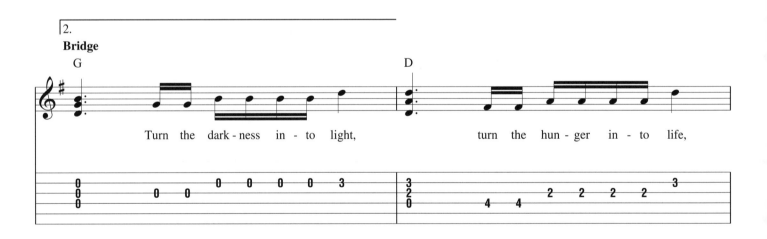

Turn the dark - ness in - to light, turn the hun - ger in - to life,

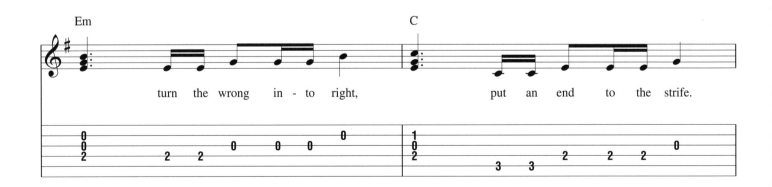

turn the wrong in - to right, put an end to the strife.

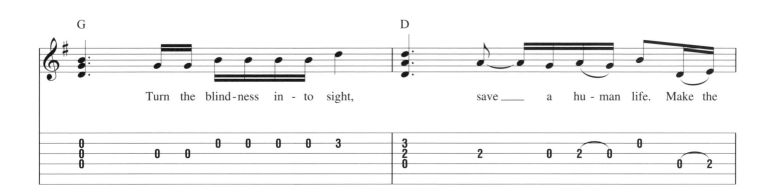

Turn the blind-ness in-to sight, save ____ a hu-man life. Make the

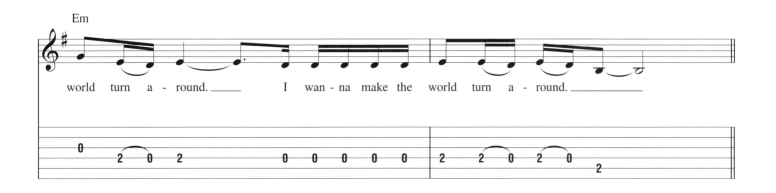

world turn a-round. ____ I wan-na make the world turn a-round. ____

Guitar Solo

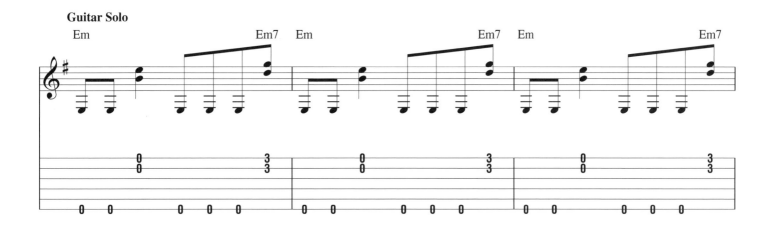

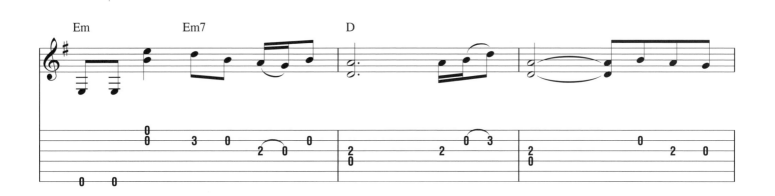

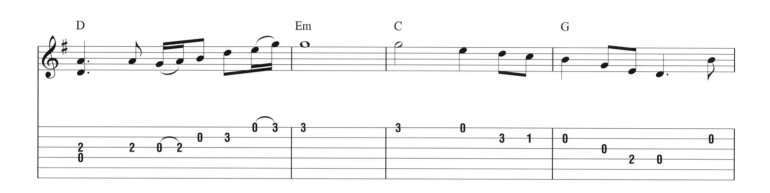

D.S. al Coda

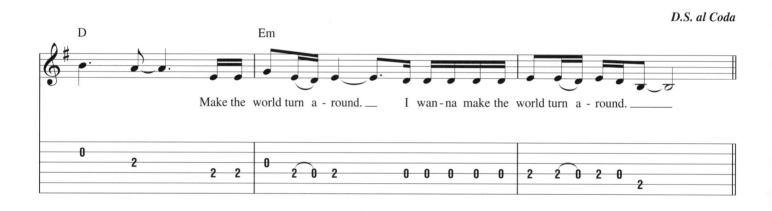

Make the world turn a - round. __ I wan-na make the world turn a - round. _____

Liv - ing in a world of jus - tice, liv - ing in a world of light.

Liv-ing in a world of free-dom, liv-ing in a world of sight.

I want to send a mes - sage to ev-'ry

boy and girl. I want to send a mes - sage a -

bout the world. We've got to build it up, stop

tear-ing it down. We've got to build it up, make the world turn a - round.

Dance Dance Dance

Words and Music by Steve Miller, Brenda Cooper and Jason Cooper

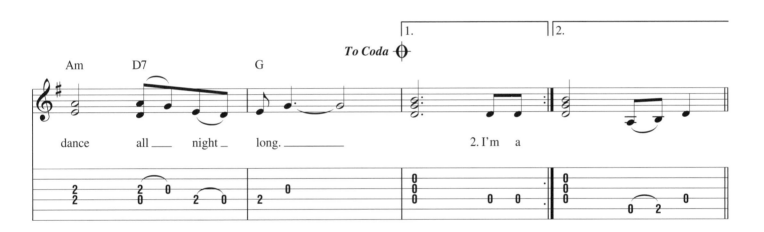

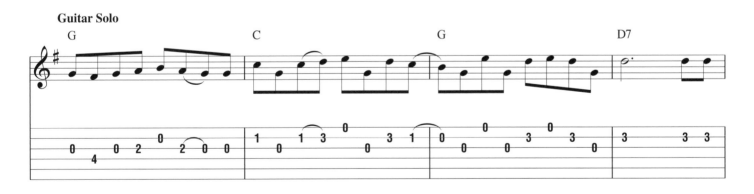

Guitar Solo

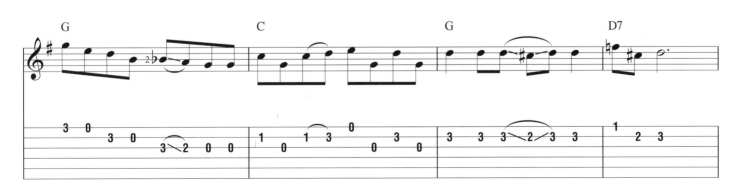

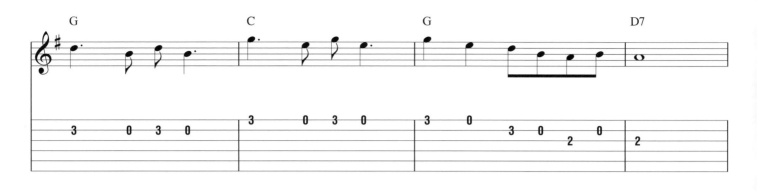

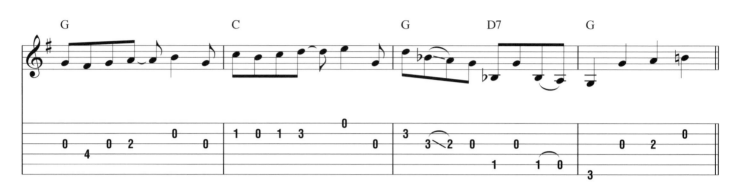

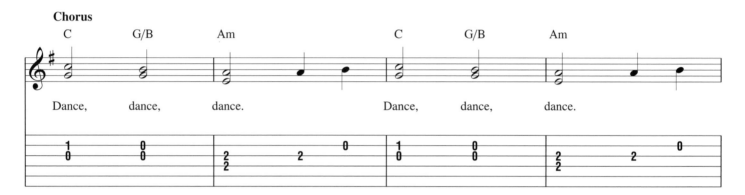

Chorus

Dance, dance, dance. Dance, dance, dance.

D.C. al Coda

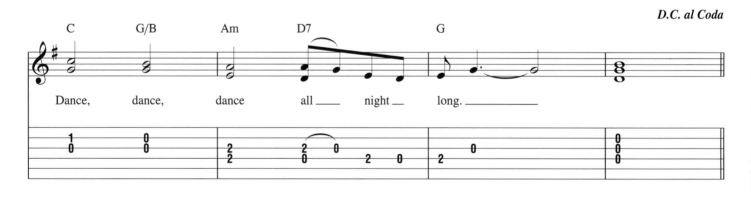

Dance, dance, dance all __ night __ long. _____

Coda

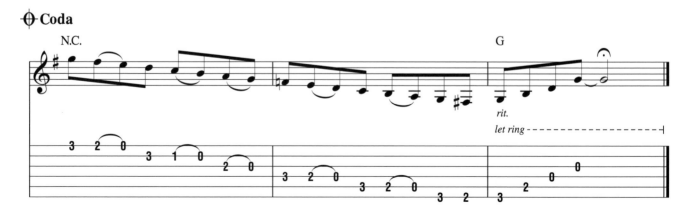

rit.

let ring - - - - - - - - - - - - - - - - - -

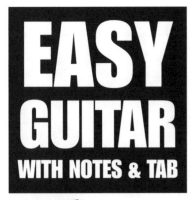

EASY GUITAR
WITH NOTES & TAB

This series features simplified arrangements with notes, TAB, chord charts, and strum and pick patterns.

MIXED FOLIOS

00309780	15 Contemporary Christian Hits	$19.95
00309781	25 Praise and Worship Favorites	$14.95
00702002	Acoustic Rock Hits for Easy Guitar	$12.95
00702166	All-Time Best Guitar Collection	$16.95
00702176	The Barney™ Songbook	$10.95
00699665	Beatles Best	$12.95
00702143	Best Chart Hits for Guitar	$9.95
00702066	Best Contemporary Hits	$9.95
00702205	The Best of Rock	$9.95
00698978	Big Christmas Collection	$16.95
00702115	Blues Classics	$10.95
00385020	Broadway Songs for Kids	$9.95
00702149	Children's Christian Songbook	$7.95
00702048	Christmas Cheer	$10.95
00702028	Christmas Classics	$7.95
00702185	Christmas Hits	$8.95
00702016	Classic Blues for Easy Guitar	$12.95
00702141	Classic Rock	$8.95
00702170	Contemporary Christian Christmas	$9.95
00702006	Contemporary Christian Favorites	$9.95
00702091	Contemporary Country Ballads	$9.95
00702065	Contemporary Women of Country	$9.95
00702191	Country Chart Hits for Guitar	$10.95
00702121	Country from the Heart	$9.95
00702085	Disney Movie Hits	$9.95
00702041	Favorite Hymns for Easy Guitar	$9.95
00702068	Forty Songs for a Better World	$10.95
00702174	God Bless America® & Other Songs for a Better Nation	$8.95
00699374	Gospel Favorites	$14.95
00702113	Grease Is Still The Word	$9.95
00702160	The Great American Country Songbook	$12.95
00702050	Great Classical Themes for Easy Guitar	$6.95
00702131	Great Country Hits of the '90s	$8.95
00702116	Greatest Hymns for Guitar	$7.95
00702130	The Groovy Years	$9.95
00702184	Guitar Instrumentals	$9.95
00702037	Hits of the '50s for Easy Guitar	$10.95
00702035	Hits of the '60s for Easy Guitar	$10.95
00702046	Hits of the '70s for Easy Guitar	$8.95
00702047	Hits of the '80s for Easy Guitar	$9.95
00702183	Hot Chart Hits for Guitar	$9.95
00702032	International Songs for Easy Guitar	$12.95
00702045	"Jailhouse Rock," "Kansas City" & Other Hits by Leiber & Stoller	$8.95
00702051	Jock Rock for Easy Guitar	$9.95
00702162	Jumbo Easy Guitar Songbook	$19.95
00702112	Latin Favorites	$9.95
00699003	The Lion King & Pocahontas for Easy Guitar	$9.95
00702061	Love Songs of the '50s and '60s for Easy Guitar	$9.95
00702062	Love Songs of the '70s and '80s for Easy Guitar	$9.95
00702063	Love Songs of the '90s for Easy Guitar	$9.95
00702138	Mellow Rock Hits	$10.95
00702147	Motown's Greatest Hits	$9.95
00702114	Movie Love Songs	$9.95
00702039	Movie Themes	$10.95
00702117	"My Heart Will Go On" & Other Top Hits	$9.95
00702026	'90s Rock for Easy Guitar	$12.95
00702067	Nutcracker Suite for Easy Guitar	$5.95
00702187	Selections from *O Brother Where Art Thou?*	$10.95
00702178	100 Songs for Kids	$12.95
02500327	Pokémon for Easy Guitar	$8.95
00702125	Praise and Worship for Guitar	$9.95
00702155	Rock Hits for Guitar	$9.95
00702135	Rock 'N' Roll Romance	$10.95

00702128	Rockin' Down the Highway	$9.95
00702137	Solid Gold Rock	$9.95
00702110	The Sound of Music	$8.95
00702042	Today's Christian Favorites for Easy Guitar	$8.95
00702124	Today's Christian Rock	$8.95
00702198	Today's Hits for Guitar	$9.95
00702171	Top Chart Hits for Guitar	$8.95
00702007	TV Tunes for Easy Guitar	$12.95
00702175	VH1's 100 Greatest Songs of Rock and Roll	$19.95
00702192	Worship Favorites	$9.95

ARTIST COLLECTIONS

00702001	Best of Aerosmith	$12.95
00702040	Best of the Allman Brothers	$9.95
00702169	Best of The Beach Boys	$10.95
00702201	The Essential Black Sabbath	$12.95
00702140	The Best of Brooks & Dunn	$10.95
00702095	Best of Mariah Carey	$10.95
00702043	Best of Johnny Cash	$12.95
00702033	Best of Steven Curtis Chapman	$12.95
00702073	Steven Curtis Chapman – Favorites	$10.95
00702090	Eric Clapton's Best	$10.95
00702086	Eric Clapton – from the album *Unplugged*	$10.95
00702053	The Best of Patsy Cline	$10.95
00702145	Best of Jim Croce	$10.95
00702122	The Doors for Easy Guitar	$10.95
00702159	Best of Genesis	$10.95
00702099	Best of Amy Grant	$9.95
00702190	The Best of Pat Green	$19.95
00702136	Best of Merle Haggard	$10.95
00702087	Best of Billy Joel	$10.95
00702088	Best of Elton John	$9.95
00702199	Norah Jones – Come Away with Me	$10.95
00702011	Best of Carole King	$12.95
00702097	John Lennon – Imagine	$9.95
00702005	Best of Andrew Lloyd Webber	$12.95
00702182	The Essential Bob Marley	$10.95
00702129	Songs of Sarah McLachlan	$12.95
00702096	Best of Nirvana	$14.95
00702197	Oasis for Easy Guitar Tab	$14.95
00699261	Oasis for Easy Guitar Tab	$14.95
00702030	Best of Roy Orbison	$12.95
00702144	The Best of Ozzy Osbourne	$12.95
00702158	Songs from Passion	$9.95
00702004	Rockin' Elvis for Easy Guitar	$9.95
00702194	Best of Twila Paris	$10.95
00702038	Elvis Presley – Songs of Inspiration	$10.95
00702139	Elvis Country Favorites	$9.95
00699415	Best of Queen for Guitar	$12.95
00702172	Richard Rodgers for Easy Guitar	$10.95
00702093	Rolling Stones Collection	$17.95
00702092	Best of the Rolling Stones	$10.95
00702196	The Best of Bob Seger	$12.95
00702010	Best of Rod Stewart	$12.95
00702150	The Best of Sting	$9.95
00702049	Best of George Strait	$10.95
00702108	The Best of Stevie Ray Vaughan	$10.95
00702123	Best of Hank Williams	$9.95
00702111	Stevie Wonder – Guitar Collection	$9.95
00702188	Essential ZZ Top	$10.95

FOR MORE INFORMATION, SEE YOUR LOCAL MUSIC DEALER, OR WRITE TO:

HAL•LEONARD® CORPORATION
7777 W. BLUEMOUND RD. P.O. BOX 13819 MILWAUKEE, WI 53213

Prices, contents and availability subject to change without notice.

www.halleonard.com

0204

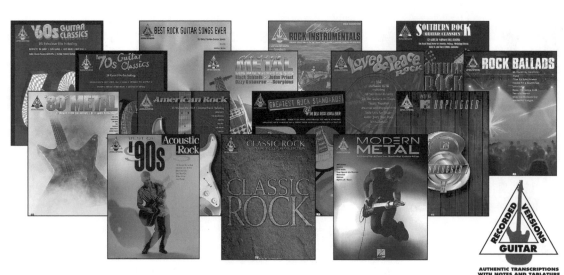